DAILY EX

managing your MONEY online

The quick, easy and effective way to manage your investments . . . wherever you are.

Trading stocks and shares online means you can manage your investments whenever, and from wherever, suits you best. And when you open an account with The Share Centre, you've access to everything you need, in one place, to make the most of that opportunity.

- Access the information you need,

- Buy and sell stocks and shares

- Monitor and manage your portfolio 24 hours a day, 7 days a week.

Your account forms the hub of your investment world ... use it to manage existing investments, track those stocks you're keeping an eye on, and to access current and historic information to help inform your investment decisions.

When it comes to dealing, your account with The Share Centre makes it simple ... and you can choose to deal immediately in 'realtime' or add your order to others for 'batch' execution.

As one of the UK's leading independent stockbrokers, you'll find our prices highly competitive ... there's a range of Accounts, each designed with different investors in mind, so you'll be sure of finding one to suit your needs, and our service is second to none.

What's more you can deal in a very wide range of UK and Overseas shares, Unit and Investment Trusts, giving you access to wider markets, and all at the same low cost.

Opening your account is just as easy; visit our website to take a virtual tour through the portfolio management service and to download your Application Form, or call us free for further information.

To find out more call 0800 800 008 or visit www.share.com

The
Share Centre
Helping you make the most of your investments

DAILY EXPRESS

managing your MONEY online

investing, saving & borrowing on the internet

steve lodge

Acknowledgements

With thanks to Stephen Pritchard for his contributions.

Publisher's note

Every possible effort has been made to ensure that the information contained in this book is accurate at the time of going to press, and the publishers and authors cannot accept responsibility for any errors or omissions, however caused. No responsibility for loss or damage occasioned to any person acting, or refraining from action, as a result of the material in this publication can be accepted by the author, the publishers or Express Newspapers.

First published in 2002

Kogan Page Ltd
120 Pentonville Road
London N1 9JN
www.kogan-page.co.uk

THE EXPRESS

© Express Newspapers 2002

British Library Cataloguing in Publication Data

A CIP record for this book is available from the British Library

ISBN 0 7494 3555 0

Typeset by Saxon Graphics Ltd, Derby
Printed and bound in Great Britain by Thanet Press Ltd, Margate

The natural choice in Kent for mortgages and savings.

Call freephone **0800 783 4248** or call in at any branch.

START HERE:

www.iii.co.uk

...is your website for everything from share trading and IPOs to unit trusts and pensions. We also provide online tools and assistance to help you make the right decision.
See for yourself, you couldn't find a better place to start

ONLINE TRADING • IPOs • UK EQUITIES • US EQUITIES • FUNDS SUPERMARK
BONDS • PENSIONS • ISAs • STAKEHOLDER PENSIONS • INVESTMENT TRUS
MORTGAGES • INSURANCE • BANKING • TRADED ENDOWMENT POLICI

interactive
investor
international
financial power is changing han

Contents

become financially connected with Sainsbury's Bank

See how you could make the most of your money, with a visit to the Sainsbury's Bank website. With just a few mouse clicks you can check out our **home and pet insurance** products, look over our **savings** rates, find an affordable way to buy a new car and see what size of **mortgage** you're eligible for. Plus, you can apply online for a Sainsbury's Bank **loan**, a **Visa** card or our great **travel insurance**. So stop by soon, and discover a bank rich in good ideas.

visit us at:
www.sainsburysbank.co.uk

Sainsbury's **Bank**

POWER TO THE INVESTOR™

Good funds cost less at TD Waterhouse

TD Waterhouse Fund Supermarket will not charge you a penny in dealing commission and we have discounted sales charges by at least 57%, and in some cases 100%.

Whether you are investing through an ISA or not, you can access hundreds of funds from the UK's top providers and diversify your portfolio across a range of sectors and countries.

Call us on 0800 169 8899 or visit www.tdwaterhouse.co.uk to find out why we have been voted the UK's Best Overall Stockbroker 2001.

Best Dealing Only Broker

UK Stockbroker Of The Year

www.tdwaterhouse.co.uk
0800 169 88 99

www. .co.uk

Pensions, investments and protection online

The Scottish Widows website gives you instant access to financial information, quotations and online applications from a name you'll recognise.

We've put full details of our range of financial products at your fingertips. You can, for example, invest directly in one of our ISAs or take out an online Stakeholder Pension Plan. You can also get an instant quote for Life Assurance or Mortgage Protection and then apply online.

To find out more, simply log on now.

SCOTTISH WIDOWS

www.scottishwidows.co.uk

Looking After Your Money Online

Banks, building societies and investment companies are all competing for your business online by providing services that allow you to look after your finances from the comfort of your own home at a time and in an environment that suits you.

You can access accounts, make transfers, pay bills, apply for and administer a mortgage or stakeholder pension plan, invest in an Individual Savings Account or unit trust and much more. You can even monitor the stockmarkets and create a virtual portfolio of shares!

With the advent of so many different facilities online, the choice of provider is ever increasing. The online companies are competing fiercely with the "clicks and mortar" banks and building societies. A "clicks and mortar" company is one that has added an online offering as a complement to its traditional high street branches. Many "clicks and mortar" banks are inviting you to do business with them on the high street, on the phone or online – whichever suits you best.

With so much choice, what should you consider when choosing an online financial company?

The usual choices
- Everything you would normally consider when choosing a bank or building society product including product features, reputation of the company and their customer service record.

How easy is their web site to use?
- You could be using their web site a lot if you administer your finances online. It is vital that you can find your way around easily and that you can get to the information quickly.
- Often the easiest sites to use are those that have a very simple, clear design and structure. They might not look as exciting as others but making changes to your account may well be a lot easier.

How much can you actually do online?
- Most companies will allow you to apply online, but will they actually allow you to make payments, transfers, change your address and so forth online once you have bought the product?

How fast and reliable is their web site?
- You don't want to have left the queues behind in the branch only to have to wait five minutes for your bank's web site to work.

By considering some of these options, you can choose an online financial provider that could mean an end to queues, giving you more time to spend doing things you enjoy!

Colin Watt, Head of E-Marketing.

rhubarb

smile customers can't stop talking about us

Our customers like us

£500 fee free overdraft

2.78% gross AER on current accounts

Is it the fact that we pay around 30 times more interest on
our current account than most of the high street banks? I
because our overdraft rate is about half of theirs (9.9% E
versus 18.4% in some cases)? Could it be because our
customers get a £500 fee free overdraft, use of 32,000
Link cash machines and the handy ability to pay cheques
by post? No, we don't think so. We think it's something e
something much, much more important. We think it's
because we're human and friendly. It may sound an od
thing for an internet bank to say, but take it from one of ou
customers who said, "I may even trust smile, a bank!" An
maybe that's why 94% of our 400,000 account holders
are prepared to recommend us to their friends.

.co
.uk

visit www.smile.co.u

from the co-operative bank

3% DEPOSIT. YOUR FIRST HOME IS JUST AROUND THE CORNER.

4.00% 5.2% APR
VARIABLE - DISCOUNTED UNTIL 30.09.03

With such a small deposit to put down, so you could borrow more, your first home could be closer than you think.

We have excellent rates to suit your needs. And Halifax offers these great extras:

- Interest calculated daily – you could save thousands
- Free Budgeting Advice from our specialist Mortgage Advisers.

So, for the shortcut to your first home, simply pick your route - pop into any branch, call us now or visit our website.

Mortgages for first time buyers

www.halifax.co.uk/mortgages

08456 00 10 00

8am to 8pm, 7 days a week

HALIFAX Always giving you extra

1
Introduction

After just a few turbulent years, the internet is now as much a part of daily life as the mobile phone. More than half of all households have internet connections. Internet access is widespread at workplaces and the e-mail an accepted form of office and business communication – even a way of doing business. Children and youngsters are clearly at ease with the new technology.

Low cost airlines – another huge new business development of recent times – already sell most of their tickets via the internet, while the likes of Amazon, the online bookseller, have grown to rival the biggest offline brands. The government even wants us to vote online. And while the initial, world-transforming internet hype of the late 1990s may have gone, the technological revolution is far from over.

High-speed broadband internet is about to massively improve video quality and the speed at which users get around the net. Instead of having to dial up to get on the internet, broadband will allow you to leave the computer on permanently and still use a phone on the same line at the same time. The convenience of always-on internet can only lead to more usage.

Wap mobile phones may have flopped and interactive TV struggled, but the internet can also be expected to establish itself in both these mediums too – the former in the form of third generation (3G) mobiles.

This book is about managing your money online – whether investing or more traditional personal finance such as banking or credit cards.

The internet could be said to be made for money. It effectively offers you direct 24-hour access to your bank's computers, allowing you to check balances and statements and move cash around. It allows users to tap into stockmarket data and news feeds, enabling investors to keep right up-to-date with changes in the value of their investments and to buy and sell immediately. It also uses computer processing power to give consumers online comparisons between financial products, allowing you to see, for example, the difference in costs over a time period or exactly how much you would save by switching. Best of all, most of the information available online is free.

The internet is giving financial consumers considerably more knowledge and power to get a better deal. The financial services industry is in parts already very competitive. But it also has long history of producing poor value and rip-offs. The relatively low costs of selling over the internet compared with having, say, high street premises is allowing financial companies to offer better deals. At the same time online consumers themselves are becoming more aware of what's available and can find the best value product from their armchairs. That in turn is piling on more pressure for companies to be competitive.

Millions of people already access their bank accounts online, while the internet has probably created at least 100,000 still-trading share investors who would never have played the markets without the net. Many net investors fell away when the bubble in technology shares burst in Spring 2000, but the dealing technology still represents a huge leap in access to information for private investors. Online fund supermarkets are also already taking a quarter of all Isa sales.

Most online purchases require the use of credit or debit cards, but internet-based cards are also developing of their own accord. Egg, Britain's biggest internet bank, has around a million credit cardholders who access their statements online.

Many of the very best value financial products are now only available online. Equally, however, the internet is not the be all and end all for financial consumers. In most cases it is simply an additional resource, not a direct replacement for existing ways of managing your money. And while it offers plenty of guidance and help in finding better deals, many people still feel the need for one-to-one financial advice, particularly on

aboutYourMoney
www.AboutYourMoney.co.uk

Empowering you to make informed financial decisions.

Compare Products
Instant Quotes
Online Applications
Advice & Information

www.AboutYourMoney.co.uk

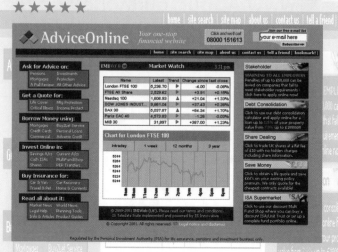

big or complex transactions like mortgages or pensions. This personalised advice hardly exists on the internet, though the advent of broadband internet should see the development of videoconferencing and therefore the ability to deliver such services.

Account aggregation services – where financial consumers can access all their accounts through one website – are also on the way. In time, too, the internet should make some of the most boring and difficult areas of money management relatively painless. Pension details will be accessible online, we will complete tax returns online, and even apply for state benefits.

This book aims to offer a practical guide to getting more from the internet, what to expect and where to look. The internet is in constant change, so by the time you read this you may find some websites and services are far more extensive than I have described, while in other cases companies will have disappeared.

Probably the biggest fear about the internet for financial consumers is security: will their money and information such as credit card details be safe? Online services insist security is a key priority and claim to be constantly looking at improvements. There is fraud on the internet and there are scams. There have been problems where consumers' accounts have been exposed to cyber-theft and no doubt hackers (or crackers as the criminal variety are termed) will pull off a massive online heist at some point. However these things happen in the real world of finance too.

More importantly still, if there is a problem then you should be covered against losses to the same degree as if the financial firm was on the high street. In the vast majority of cases that means you should be fully compensated for thefts from your online accounts or misuse of your credit card; you should even be protected in the event of the financial collapse of any (reputable) organisation you are dealing with.

If your credit card is misused, your maximum exposure is £50, and most card companies will waive even this amount. If your bank, broker or insurer goes bust, an industry compensation scheme will step in to cover the majority of losses.

The relevant chapters explain how you are protected in more detail. But consumers also need to be sensible about the organisations they deal with and about keeping safe the personal information that could be used to access their accounts. The Financial Services Authority (FSA), the chief financial watchdog has a useful 'consumer update' on e-commerce at www.fsa.gov.uk/consumer/whats_new/updates/e_commerce/index – which is full of tips about internet financial services and how to protect yourself online.

Here is an edited version of that guide:

What's different about buying online?

Some things may work a little differently from what you're used to, or from what you expect. For example:

- You may have more passwords or PIN numbers to remember.
- You may need to follow hyperlinks between different web pages or to scroll down menus to access important information such as terms and conditions or, for investment products, the key features document.
- When you're on a firm's website, it may not be obvious where it is based.
- You may not be able to access the website sometimes. In some cases, this might simply be because the firm has taken their website down at quiet times for maintenance, or it could be because there are a lot of people trying to use the firm's website at the same time.
- You may come across things like chat rooms and bulletin boards, which are internet sites where people exchange views and news, for example, on the stockmarket. This can feel friendly like talking in the pub but, as with chatting socially, the information is not always accurate or reliable.

Using online services

When you're looking for financial products and services in the high street you usually get a better deal by shopping around. The same is true of looking for products and services online. However, there are a few additional things you might want to add to your checklist for shopping around on the internet.

- Before dealing with firms you've never heard of, check whether they're authorised (see below).
- If you're going to buy online or use a service online, consider how easy a firm's website is to use – how easy is it to find your way around? Can you find the information you need?
- Read the product details, terms and conditions, key features, etc before you commit yourself. And don't press send or click to continue until you are sure.
- Print off or save information because you may not get a paper copy sent to you. For example, print off the terms and conditions – they may have changed if you go back to the website later.
- If possible, print off forms you've filled in to keep for your own records – you may need them if you have to make a claim later.
- If you fill in forms online, check them carefully – drop-down menus may have default options already filled in which you might want to change. For example, the default might be an interest-only mortgage, but you might be looking for, and need to select, a repayment mortgage.
- If you receive paperwork, check it when it arrives.
- Get in touch with the firm straight away if you find a mistake.
- Don't go ahead unless you are entirely happy with the service, deal, terms, etc.

Safety and security tips

The internet is a public network so it's important to take a few precautions to try and ensure you know who you're dealing with and to keep your money secure. The vast majority of online financial firms are genuine and authorised firms. But it is possible for fraudsters to set up a dummy or look-a-like site so that they can try and get people to hand over banking details, credit card numbers and other security information. Check out the following if you're using online financial services:

- Check that you've logged on to a firm's genuine website. Some dummy or bogus websites may deliberately use a name or web address very similar to that of a genuine firm. Don't continue if you think there is anything odd about the website. Always check the web address you have typed is the correct one before providing your personal security information and carrying out a transaction.
- Check that the website provides information that identifies the firm. This should include a physical (postal) address and telephone number for the firm. Check this contact information using other sources, for example, Directory Enquiries or Yellow Pages.
- Check the firm you're dealing with is authorised. An authorised firm must meet set standards before it is allowed to do business. You are only protected by the UK complaints and compensation schemes if you deal with an authorised firm or its appointed representatives. Financial firms in any country in the European Economic Area (EEA) can offer products and services in any other EEA country – firms are regulated in the home country but must also meet standards that have been agreed across all EEA countries.

To check if a firm is authorised call the FSA Consumer Helpline on 0845 606 1234. There is also a user-friendly online service available. To find out more about it go to the FSA Firm Check Service at www.fsa.gov.uk/consumer/fcs/index

- Check the details of overseas firms. The web's full name is the World Wide Web – and it is world-wide. You may find services offered by firms based in countries outside of the EEA. If you are thinking of doing business with an overseas firm, check if there are contact details so that you can find out how it is regulated and if there are complaints and compensation schemes in case anything goes wrong.

- Comparing information. The internet makes it much easier to access products and services from different countries. When you're looking at information about products online, remember that not all information will be put together on the same basis and not all products will be directly comparable. For example, illustrations of what you might get back could be based on different assumptions about how an investment might perform, and different products could have different tax treatments in different countries.

Check the connection between you and the firm is secure. You should only provide bank details, passwords, PIN numbers, credit card details and other security information to firms that encrypt the data so no one else can read it. You can check the connection is secure by:

- asking the firm if your transaction data is encrypted (in code so that people outside of the firm you are dealing with can't intercept or read what is being sent between you and the firm);
- looking for the firm's security policy on the website to see if data is encrypted;

- looking for a closed-padlock or other security symbol on your screen or 'https' in the left-hand side of the web address box (instead of 'http') to indicate encryption is taking place.

Keep your information private, safe and secure. Use your passwords, credit card information, PIN numbers and other security information carefully. For example:

- Choose your passwords carefully – don't use obvious things like your account name, date of birth, or the word 'password'.
- Try and ensure your passwords and other log-in details are unique and could not easily be guessed by other people.
- Try and memorise your passwords and other security information – try not to write them down (others might find and use them).
- If you do need to write them down because you can't remember them all, don't leave them where they can easily be found (for example, by your computer) and don't write them down in the same place. It is also important to disguise them so it isn't obvious what the number or password is for.
- Do not store your password on the PC, it's much safer to type in your password each time you access the service.
- Try to avoid accessing sensitive information in a public place – if you need to do so, whether at work, in an internet café, a library, etc, make sure no one is looking over your shoulder at the computer screen.
- If you do access sensitive information in a public place, never leave the computer unattended, and close down the internet browser program when you are finished to clear any security information from the PC.
- If you think someone else knows your security information, tell the financial firm you're dealing with straight away – when you contact the firm they'll tell you what to do.

The safest way to operate your online accounts is to keep your passwords and PIN numbers confidential. However, some services ask you to let them know your password – if you want to use these services and you haven't checked with your original service provider that this is okay, you may risk losing money if an unauthorised transaction takes place. For example, account aggregation services may ask for your passwords (account aggregation services allow you to view all information from your different online accounts on one website – see Chapter 8). Always check with your service provider if it is okay to give your password to another firm before using the latter's services – if in doubt, don't give your password to anyone else.

Keep your computer safe from unfriendly software such as viruses. A computer virus is a program that could stop your computer working properly. Some virus programs can record what you type, which could give them the information they need to access your online financial accounts. Viruses can be sent as files attached to e-mails. You can help prevent virus problems by:

- Deleting e-mails with attachments before your read them if you don't know and trust the person that sent you the e-mail.
- Installing good anti-virus software to check for viruses before you open files – check out computer retailers and computer magazines for further information.
- Keep your anti-virus software up-to-date – new viruses are developed regularly, so keep up by downloading updates from the manufacturer's web-site.

How to get started

You don't have to have a home computer to access the internet. Many working people will be connected at their workplace, while plenty of public libraries offer access (sometimes free). Internet cafés are also fairly common on high streets – particularly in major towns and cities.

If you can get away with using the internet at work for your finances, then that's not a bad option. Computer technology is improving all the time – so as soon you buy your own machine it will in effect be out-of-date – and chances are your employer will have better technology and internet connections than you will want to shell out for. Failing that, just bite the bullet and buy anyway. Perfectly good internet-ready computers are available from around £500 these days – even from supermarkets like Tesco. You won't get the latest laptop computer, but many experts will say that's just as well – not only do you get more for your money from a 'desktop' sized computer, but they're also better ergonomically speaking (try writing a lot on a fiddly laptop keypad, as this book was!).

Most modern computers will come internet-ready with modem (for connecting to the internet via your telephone socket) and the necessary internet software. This will include an Internet Service Provider (ISP), which is your gateway to the web. However, you don't need to stick with the ISP you're given and it may well be worth investigating alternative providers – particularly as ISP set-up discs are freely available.

Quality of connection and cost are probably the two main issues to consider with an ISP. The internet can be slow to get around, difficult to connect to, and you will lose your connection from time to time. None of this is fun.

Asking for recommendations from friends or colleagues is one way of finding a decent ISP – or try Which? reports or similar computer magazines. Or just try the ISP you have and stick with it until it starts to let you down.

Even if the provided ISP account itself is 'free' you will still have to pay phone charges for the time you are online. If you are going to use the internet to any degree you should look at a flat-rate package, which typically gives you unlimited access for around £15 a month.

Broadband internet offers faster speeds and is always-on – meaning you don't have to waste time connecting every time you want to go on the net and you can also use your phone from the same line at the same time. However, broadband currently costs more.

Shortcuts to managing money online

This book aims to be a practical guide to managing your money online. As well as telling you what the internet has to offer, the hope is it will serve as a guidebook and map as you actually navigate around the web.

There are literally thousands of financial websites out there in cyberspace, and hundreds are detailed or listed in this book. Just as you shouldn't take up the first financial offer you see in a bank branch or receive in junk mail without investigating the alternatives, equally you should investigate the world of online money at your own pace. But for readers looking for a 'quick fix' improvement in their finances – and for those who don't know where to begin – here are ten top websites and services to start with:

1.   Sign on with AOL as your ISP (Internet Service Provider). Its Your Money channel (my employer!) is the best of its kind and provides useful links to other websites and services (www.aol.co.uk or 0800 376 5599).

2.   FT Your Money (www.ftyourmoney.com). The most authoritative personal finance website around, with links to other www.ft.com services. A word of warning, though: the FT is looking at charging for access.

3.   Google (www.google.co.uk). An excellent search engine for finding other websites. Start by finding your bank's website and see if you like its service.

4.   Moneyfacts (www.moneyfacts.co.uk). The 'rate bible' of the personal finance industry, this website will give you the latest rates, product features and performance of a whole range of financial products.

5.   IF (www.if.com). Intelligent Finance, an online/phone banking arm of the Halifax, probably offers the best overall value of any online bank, in part due to its offsetting of debts against deposits to give you a better interest rate deal.

6. Egg (www.egg.com). The Pru-owned online bank has consistently offered best-buy credit cards and savings accounts. Its lively website underlines how Egg has quickly become one of the strongest financial brands around – on- and offline.

7. Hometrack (www.hometrack.co.uk). Probably the most detailed house price checker service on the internet.

8. Charcolonline (www.charcolonline.co.uk). Britain's leading mortgage broker should be able to help you find a cheaper home loan, potentially saving you thousands of pounds. Charcol's website also covers investments, pensions, and insurance.

9. FSA (www.fsa.gov.uk). The boring bit! The website of Britain's chief financial watchdog. Excellent reference material and information, nevertheless.

10. Hargreaves Lansdown (www.hargreaveslansdown.co.uk). Yet to embrace as much interactivity as other fund supermarkets, but Hargreaves still gives the biggest discounts on many investment funds and Isas.

Finally, while I have tried to explain as much jargon (internet and financial) as I go, Chapter 14 has an A–Z jargonbuster for further help.

2

News and Information Sources

The internet offers an extraordinary amount of information, most of it still free. In fact there is so much information available on the net that the challenge is to find what you want and get it in a manageable form.

If you are after up-to-the-minute financial news (or up-to-the-second share prices), the internet has it. Personalised information and news on particular financial subjects can be e-mailed to you periodically, while special e-mail alerts will tell you when, say, a share has hit a certain price. Equally if you want to compare two financial products, or find the best according to certain criteria, then you should be able to find a service on the web that will do it for you.

Most of the main newspapers, as well as the BBC, are on the internet in some shape or form – whether it is simply the paper's existing editorial 'content' or a more enhanced service. The BBC, for example, offers an excellent, constantly-updated news service on the web. But while many of these websites from established players are very good, and for some people will even serve as an alternative to traditional newspapers or other media, few have found a way of making any money. Advertising revenues have been low, production and running costs often high. Consequently, the trend is increasingly towards charging users for access.

Compared with say the financial pages of a newspaper, financial websites will also offer their users more interactivity. As well as providing information, product comparisons and guidance, many websites will allow you to transact – whether, for example, opening an account, checking a balance or taking out insurance. In some cases the interactive element is limited simply to registering for information to be sent to you. Other websites will have built-in application forms, 'shops' or links through to financial companies. Many also have generic help-tools for working out, for example, what a particular loan would cost you or for monitoring the performance of investment portfolios.

The degree of interactivity and transactional integration varies considerably. Many of the traditional media players have stuck to information only – whether consciously or not – while the newer online brands have understandably been more commercial and innovative in their approach.

Inevitably this has meant some blurring of the boundaries between traditional information providers and commercial entities – a change that is not necessarily problematic, but that consumers should at least be aware of when on the web. At best, online services give wholly impartial information and guidance at no cost and then let you transact. At worst financial companies have found a new way of dressing up their hard-sell.

News and general information websites

Daily Express/Sunday Express
Although at the time of writing the Express does not have a website, it is well worth following their financial pages for the most up-to-date and informative financial advice.

BBC
The BBC has one of the very best general news websites. Finance-wise, it has sections for Business, Your Money (personal finance), Market Data and a useful Q&A Basics area, among others. For news, start at http://news.bbc.co.uk/ The main website at www.bbc.co.uk also has links to web pages for programmes such as Hard Cash, Your Money or Your Life, and Working Lunch. There are also video and audio clips promoted across its service.

Financial Times
The most authoritative financial and business newspaper in the UK, the FT has invested many millions in a variety of web services. www.ft.com is the main brand and contains links to all its other services, including a personal finance website (www.ftyourmoney.com), FT Investor (www.ft.com/investor) (for investors) and Investors Chronicle magazine (www.investorschronicle.co.uk) (up for sale at the time of writing).

FT Your Money has a number of useful tools for finding, among others, cheaper insurance and a better value stockbroker (http://ftyour-money.ft. com/FTym/brokerfinder).

The FT's online empire offers something for a wide range of users – business people, investors and financial consumers. Much of its well-regarded Weekend Money personal finance section (in the Saturday paper) can be found at www.ftyourmoney.com and elsewhere.

But the one big problem with the FT's extensive web coverage is that it is planning to charge for access (the IC already charges for areas such as stockmarket tips). Details were unavailable at the time of writing, but some content is expected to remain free.

Wall Street Journal (www.wsj.com)
In effect, an American Financial Times, the Journal only offers limited content on the web and has been successfully charging for full access for some time.

Economist magazine (www.economist.com)
Some free, some subscription-only content.

This Is Money (www.thisismoney.co.uk)
The financial website of Associated Newspapers.

www.ananova.com
A useful newswire service which has up-to-date business, stockmarket, and personal finance news, including an amusing 'business quirkies' section whose recent articles included 'Businesses blame cats and budgies for late bill payments' and 'Jobless people sent bowling to find work'.

Guardian Money (www.guardian.co.uk/Money/)

While not the most obvious first choice for a financial newspaper, the Guardian arguably has the best web operation of any paper. Its Money section carries financial articles from the Guardian and Observer newspapers as well as original content. There are also a number useful interactive calculators:

- for comparing utility prices;
- for working out mortgage repayments as well as how much you can borrow;
- for working out required pension contributions;
- for working out how much you could save by consolidating debts into a single monthly payment;
- for comparing savings and investment growth and how returns might vary.

Daily Telegraph/Sunday Telegraph (www.money.telegraph.co.uk)

The Telegraph was the first British newspaper to go online back in 1994 – eons ago in internet time! The City and business coverage of both newspapers is highly regarded. The Money sections are also well read. The website carries all these sections as well as having a useful archive. Again, the concern is that the newspaper is looking at charging for access.

Times/Sunday Times (www.thetimes.co.uk)

Similar format to the Telegraph.

Bloomberg (www.bloomberg.co.uk)

The business news and information company of the mayor of New York (Michael Bloomberg), its web service is really aimed at business people and sophisticated investors. Gives real-time data and up-to-the-minute news.

AOL

For users of its ISP service, AOL probably has the best and most extensive financial coverage of its type around. Aimed at the mid-market, it is well-designed and accessible. As well as pulling together 'best of breed' editorial content from a range of internet 'partners', AOL produces its own features as well. It also has a user-friendly My Portfolio tool for monitoring the value of investments. The media giant's portal at www.aol.co.uk only gives limited content.

Freeserve

Freeserve, AOL's arch-rival, also gives its ISP customers financial content.

Yahoo (http://uk.finance.yahoo.com/)

E-mail users of the popular Yahoo portal can get a variety of financial and other news.

The Motley Fool (www.fool.co.uk)

If, despite your best efforts to get to grips with the world of finance, it remains complex, confusing and, well, boring, then the Motley Fool may be for you. The UK version of an American service, The Fool's big plus point is its colloquial, jokey approach. Some may find the idea of 'foolish ways of investing' and 'fool school' a little irritating, however.

Other services

There have long been too many financial companies selling too many financial products, and consumers have struggled to make even simple comparisons of what offers the best deal or performance. The internet has a number of directories as well as product database websites that will help you find particular types of financial companies (effectively an online financial Yellow Pages) or compare rates and returns.

Here are some of the general financial websites. Later chapters covering individual financial areas also include websites that compare particular product types.

Moneyfacts (www.moneyfacts.co.uk)
Moneyfacts has long been the industry bible for savings and mortgage rates, with its excellent monthly magazine and as the provider of many newspapers' best-buy tables. It now has a similarly comprehensive directory website that covers savings accounts, mortgages, investments, credit cards and other personal finance products. Combines best buy-style tables with A to Z listings, which in theory should allow you to find the best deals as well as checking up on what particular companies are offering. You can't buy through the website, but can click through to companies' websites. Its Information Channel also covers other areas such as travel and jobs through linked services.

Blay's Guides (www.blays.co.uk)
A competitor of Moneyfacts. In some ways its online best-buy tables are better, though the overall service is not as comprehensive in terms of the range of financial products covered.

Find (Financial Information Net Directory) (www.find.co.uk)
Probably the most well-known online directory of financial companies (rather than specific products). Claims to have thousands of links to financial companies and products. Aims to show all UK financial websites and also includes sites that don't let you buy online. Makes its money by charging for advertising and listings, like the Yellow Pages does, rather than from transactions.

www.moneymile.com is another directory.

If you can't find a particular company or website, a search engine such as **Google** (www.google.co.uk) should be able to locate it for you.

A recent report by *Which?* magazine noted that websites that compare financial products usually have disclaimers stating that the information on the site might not be accurate or up-to-date. It recommended comparing the results and recommendations from a couple of sites so that you can be reasonably confident that you are making an informed choice. Equally it noted that some websites have unique deals that aren't available anywhere else.

The following product comparison websites are more geared towards transactions:

Moneysupermarket (www.moneysupermarket.com)
Claims to cover 3,600 mortgages from 180 lenders and 65 personal loans from 40 different companies, as well as credit cards, savings, current accounts, offshore savings, travel insurance and private medical insurance.

Moneynet (www.moneynet.co.uk)
Claims more than 450 loans from 55 companies, also credit cards, savings, and medical, motor, travel and home insurance.

Moneyextra (www.moneyextra.com)
Owned by Bristol & West, the former building society, it also offers phone-based advice and information.

3

Banking and Saving

Online banking has been one of the internet's success stories. Industry estimates vary but between 4 million and 6 million Britons have some sort of access to their bank accounts over the internet. This is expected to grow to half the adult population by 2004, according to the research company Forrester.

Convenience and better interest rates are the attractions of online banking. Instead of queuing in a bank branch, most day-to-day transactions can be carried out over the internet in just a few minutes. Most banks' websites are open 24 hours a day, which makes it much easier to manage finances in the evening or at the weekend. Combine that access with cashpoint withdrawals (and deposits, in many cases) as well being able to pay in cheques via the post, and there is no reason why you need step foot in a bank branch again. Nor is it necessary to switch to an internet bank: all the main UK banks now offer their own online services. For most current account customers, setting up internet access to their existing current account is the best way to try out online banking. There is no charge for this, but allow at least two to three weeks for all the paperwork to arrive.

Once online, most of the banks' websites work in the same way and offer broadly similar services. After logging on – you will need a user name or number, a password and up to three other pieces of identity information – most banks show a screen detailing a customer's accounts and current balances. Double-clicking on the account should bring up a list of recent transactions, rather like a conventional statement. Depending on the bank, the system might display transactions going back a year or more, or just since the last paper statement.

Other useful features of online banking are transfers and bill payments. Online banking supports both regular payments, such as standing orders, and one-off transfers and bills. In fact, the distinction is less than clear, as it is possible to pre-programme payments as far as six months ahead. Some banks provide lists of account details for common bills, such as gas, electricity and phone, and most let users store details for bills they pay regularly.

However, despite their 'open all hours' nature, internet banks do still have to work within the existing banking system. So generally transfers and payments, as well as cheques, will still take the standard three working days to go through or clear. But within the bank, transfers should be easier and take place on the same day, if not instantly – so minimising any loss of interest.

The high street banks do not limit their online services to current accounts, but can link in savings accounts too. Barclays, for example, puts all its customers' accounts online when they register, but banks' policies do vary; you might need to sign separate forms for any joint accounts.

Having all your accounts online is useful, making it convenient for moving money into higher-paying accounts. However, the clearing banks rarely offer the best deals on interest rates or bank charges. This accolade is usually won by one of the newer banks offering services either entirely or mostly via the internet.

Higher interest rates

Better interest rates are the most headline-grabbing reason to go online. Banks such as Smile, Cahoot and Intelligent Finance (IF) have challenged the traditional operators by paying attractive interest rates for customers in credit, and undercutting their rivals on overdraft charges too. The exact deals on offer vary constantly, so it is worth shopping around. Bear in mind too that some of the newer banks have strict

I'm not like normal people – my working day starts when most people are going home and thinking about dinner and bedtime! Given the unsociable hours that I work, I need a bank that's open all hours – with products and services that can fit in around my lifestyle. I'm no techno whizz kid so I used to think that banking over the Internet would be really complicated. I'd heard it wasn't safe, and I never thought that I would take the plunge and use technology to make my money work for me. That was until I discovered Open Plan from The Woolwich – a newly upgraded web-bank that helps me to be smart when managing my money.

Open Plan makes managin

At the times when I can't go in the branch or pick up the phone, I know I can go online and manage my money. I can log on from work, or from my home PC at any time of the night or day. And it's really easy to use and find my way around. The Woolwich has made Open Plan even easier to benefit from by talking to all kinds of people who've given fresh ideas about how to make banking online as clear and simple as possible. They really listen to their customers and take on board their suggestions.

And you don't have to be a night watchman to find this useful. My sister-in-law always used to pop into the branch at lunchtime but now she just finds the web more convenient. She's even getting into mobile banking on her WAP phone. That's what's great about Open Plan – you're not restricted to one method of banking, you can mix and match to suit your needs.

Before I started with Open Plan my finances were a bit of a mess. I never knew what my balance was, or whether cheques had cleared and I was forever forgetting to pay bills. Now though, I'm totally in control. My bill payments are all scheduled in and I can check my balance and standing orders at the click of a button.

open plan from THE WOOLWICH

I've even started to make money – without having to lift a finger! Basically, if the money in my account goes above a set level it's automatically transferred into my savings account overnight – and I wake up knowing my money's earning more interest. Similarly, when my current account is running low, money is swept back, topping it up to cover my cheques and other payments. I just sit back and let it all happen – knowing that my money is really working for me.

Open Plan makes saving as easy as possible – I've virtually paid for next year's summer holiday already by taking advantage of their unique 'saving pots'. You can open up to 12 pots – and name them whatever you like, from 'Christmas presents' to 'new car' – and you get the interest on the combined balance of all your savings.

As well as being free of charge, I also have the peace of mind that my Open Plan account is totally secure. The Woolwich uses all sorts of advanced technology to ensure the safety of your account. And it also guarantees to cover any losses in the unlikely event of a security breach.

Well, I've spent a couple of minutes online now – time to get back to work. Everything is so simple with Open Plan online banking – I can't believe I used to bank any other way.

ur money as easy as possible

For an online demonstration, or just to find out more about Open Plan from The Woolwich visit www.thewoolwich.co.uk Or visit your local branch Or call **0845 607 1111**

Today's busy lifestyles and advancements in communication technology mean that more of us are choosing to bank on the move in the most convenient way. But just what are the different banking options available? And which ones will work best for you? To guide you through this changing landscape, we take a look at the new ways people are managing their money and speak to six people who are making banking fit round their lifestyles.

Online banking

More of us bank online in the UK than anywhere else in Europe – an estimated 7.5 million at the end of 2001, and that's expected to rise above 13 million by 2005.

Banking on the internet allows you to access your account at any time of the day or night without having to visit a local branch. Managing money between accounts and arranging to pay bills is straightforward and the system allows you to view and change standing orders easily. Some banks offer added benefits to online customers – like The Woolwich who will automatically transfer money you're not using above a set level from your current to your savings account to make sure you earn more interest on your money.

"It's all about taking control of your finances," says graphic designer, Steve Kennedy. "Before I started banking online I never had a clue what state my balance was in, whether bills had been debited from my account or cheques cleared. Now I feel totally in control.

"Online banking gives me the feeling of being at the cutting edge and is also totally functional. I also enjoy peace of mind of being with a bank like The Woolwich that's got a strong heritage and there's a total security guarantee too."

WAP

Over a million of us enjoy mobile banking from a WAP. Banking on the go certainly appeals to working mum, Kate Berry: "In between looking after two children and my job as a sales rep, I don't have time for traditional banking. That's why WAP banking is ideal for me. I can check my balance while

I'm waiting to pick the kids up, pay a bill between meetings or transfer money when I'm in the back of a cab. I can also keep an eye on my finances when I travel abroad."

Interactive Digital Television

The age of banking from the armchair is here. Viewers can check their balance, monitor transactions and use an on-screen financial planner in the usual sound and picture format, and go online for information or do transactions via a phone link into a free digital set-top box.

Football coach, Carl Cox, is converted: "I first got digital TV for the sport – now I find it's great for banking. I'm on the go all day and haven't got the time to go to a bank. I just want to relax when I get in but having sound finances is also important. Now I can manage my money before watching the game or after Eastenders – all from my sofa – it's ideal."

Talking to real people

All high street banks allow you to manage your account over the phone. George Gardiner a retired school teacher says: "I do like the personal touch – that's why I like to speak to someone over the phone or go into my branch. I am becoming a bit of an internet fan in my retirement though, and will definitely investigate online banking."

So today's banks offer a range of options to suit our different lifestyle needs. And you don't necessarily have to choose one banking channel over another, but take advantage of all the options available, like newly-weds Justine and John Taylor: "With our full time jobs and house hunting we're always on the go – so online and WAP banking is great. As well as being convenient it's made us be much more efficient with our money.

"But sometimes we really need to get face to face advice from our branch. We bank with The Woolwich and their independent financial advisers have been great. At the end of the day, it's all about being able to manage our money around our lives – and not being restricted by branch opening times. We now have so many options open to us. It's perfect."

Getting to grips with your finances online

The chimes of Big Ben. The clink of champagne glasses. The dawn of a New Year. And as you reached for the Alka Seltzer on New Year's Day you may well have decided that one of your New Year's resolutions would be that in 2002 you would finally get on top of your finances and sort them out.

That promise to yourself may seem a long and distant one now, and let's face it, there are other more exhilarating things to do. But help is at hand from norwichunion.com.

norwichunion.com was designed to help people take a more active role in managing their finances online. More and more people like you are turning to the internet to manage their money. And why not? It's convenient, secure and lets you decide what to do.

At norwichunion.com you'll find a wealth of free interactive financial planning tools and impartial money guides to help you work out what you may need to do become better off.

Kick off with the 60 second wealth check which'll give you a summary of the current state of your finances in the five key areas of financial planning.

Keep up-to-speed with what you're currently worth with My wealth manager. It'll show you what you earn and what you spend, what you own and what you owe. Plus, it can automatically update the values of your fund and share investments at a click of a button.

These tools are free to use and by registering at www.norwichunion.com you will be able to save your information securely.

Our new Fund Supermarket ISA (operated by nusof.com limited) provides you with a better way of investing in an ISA. You can choose to invest your ISA money in up to 14 funds from around 70 from some of the best fund managers in the business all at initial charges that are up to 75% less than you would normally pay*. Each fund has a prestigious Standard & Poor's A, AA or AAA rating which means you can pick from the cream of the crop.

And, if you have a portfolio of shares our online share dealing service could be just what you need to build and manage a profitable portfolio. You have the ability to buy and sell shares using real time prices in a secure environment.

norwichunion.com was named as "Innovation of the Year" and "Online Provider of the Year" at the Investor's Week Online Personal Finance Awards 2001 – so visit us at www.norwichunion.com.

*Source Norwich Union: Modal initial average charge of funds in the Norwich Union Fund Supermarket ISA is 1.25%. Modal average quoted by the fund managers for these funds is 5.25%

Norwich Union Wealth Management Limited is regulated by the Financial Services Authority for investment business

Now for the first time in the UK, Citibank have launched a brand new service called **"My Accounts"** that enables you to view your online accounts on one page.

Check your bank, share dealing and credit card details.

You can even view your air miles and email!

It's FREE of charge and accessed with just one secure password.

You don't even have to bank with us.

All your accounts, all on one page, all with one password.

Register today with **My Accounts** on:

policies on credit checks and even minimum income levels, so not every-one will be able to switch.

Using the internet to find a better savings rate is straightforward. Again, the new banks usually beat their branch-based rivals for simple savings accounts, and also for cash Isas. But do not rule out the older-established banks or building societies. More banks and societies are offering online savings accounts as well as, or instead of, postal accounts. And the rates will almost always be better than a branch-based account.

For some consumers, however, the idea of managing an account entirely over the internet is still a step too far. Security fears and, to a lesser extent, reliability of service are what have held back many bank customers.

Security

While technical glitches can – and do – continue to happen with websites, security is much less of a problem than newcomers to online banking often fear. The online banking systems of the UK banks are secure, relying on a combination of advanced technology and basic measures such as special PIN numbers and personal information to iden-tify authorised users.

There is little reason to suspect that online banking is generally any less secure for day-to-day use than phone banking or dealing with the bank through the branch or cashpoint.

There are some areas, though, where it could be a worry. Banks use secure connections (known as SSL or secure socket layer) for connections between the user's computer and their central systems. It's easy to spot a secure connection, as the web address will start with https:// and your internet page will show a key or padlock symbol at the bottom. It would be very hard for a criminal or hacker to break the current 128 bit SSL technology and even if they did, the effort it would take to break into an individual's online banking screen is unlikely to be worth the trouble.

Open a branch at home today

Armchair Banking

You can do your banking from the comfort of your armchair with NatWest OnLine Banking.
Once you've logged on it's like having your own branch in your living room, bedroom, office or wherever it is you keep your PC.
Here are just some of the things you can do from your PC:

· View balances and mini statements – showing you the most recent transactions on whichever account you choose
· Make transfers between your NatWest accounts
· View and access up to six months of statements online
· Pay bills
· Set up and view standing orders

We also have a number of features which should help you run your current account more efficiently. These include:

· The option to download current, savings and loan account data onto your computer and use financial planning tools
· An on-screen calculator to help you manage budgets
· The opportunity to personalise your account names – so those savings for home improvements can be kept in your 'DIY account', the savings for your child's higher education in 'University funds' etc.

Application's easy

To apply, simply visit www.natwest.com and click on the apply button under NatWest OnLine Banking, quoting reference EXP03.
If you don't have Internet access, pick up the free NatWest OnLine ISP CD-ROM in any NatWest branch. Alternatively call us on 0845 602 5588 and we'll send you one.

(Lines are open 8am to 8pm Monday to Friday and 9am to 6pm Saturdays. Calls are charged at the local rate.)
We may monitor and record your phone calls with us in order to maintain and improve our service.
NatWest OnLine Banking via the Internet is free to all NatWest account holders although your Internet Service Provider may charge you for accessing the service.

National Westminster Bank Plc, Registered Office: 135 Bishopsgate, London, EC2M 3UR.
Registered number: 929027, England.

www.nationwide.co.uk – the easy way to make the most of your money... and your PC!

At www.nationwide.co.uk there's something for everyone, from managing your current account, savings and even your mortgage to getting quotes and applying for a wide range of award winning financial products including personal loans and travel, car and home insurance. You can check your balance, transfer money to other people and pay bills. This is complemented by services available via the latest in Internet devices – Pocket PC (PDA), WAP mobile phone and Internet TV.

The site is simple and secure. The Internet Banking service recently won a "Secure E-Business Award" at the Computer Weekly E-Business Excellence awards for the innovative & effective way it tackles security issues. In addition, users of the Internet Banking service automatically benefit from the Society's Internet Banking Promise.

The Society is preparing to launch a redesigned site by early summer including new clearer menus and screens, along with improved help reflecting where you are. Users will also be able to decide which page is loaded first and print and download statements for the first time.

Anyone can visit the website at www.nationwide.co.uk. Nationwide wants everyone to be able to take advantage of the online services on offer. If you're unsure in taking your first step, Nationwide branches will also help you get started for the first time with an Internet Banking lesson.

Go online now – it's easy.

INTERNET BANKING   Nationwide

Put your PC to better use.
Go to www.nationwide.co.uk

Are you just playing around with your PC? You are, if you're not banking over the Internet with us. With a Nationwide Current Account you can manage your money just how you want. It's quick. It's secure. And it's so easy.

Plus we don't charge for day-to-day services, or for arranging an overdraft. And you'll earn ten times more interest on credit balances than you'll get from most other current accounts.

So use your mouse and visit us today.

Nationwide. Underlining the difference

www.nationwide.co.uk | ☎ 08457 30 20 10 | 🏠 or just call in

| Banking | Credit Card | Insurance | Investments | Loans | Mortgages | Pensions | Savings |

Where users are at more risk is if they use computers in a public place, such as an internet café, or use a shared machine at work. Home users should never store access codes and PINs on their PCs, either in e-mail or word-processed documents, let alone as 'Post-it' notes stuck to the screen. Treat your online account information as you would your cash card details. However, there is always a chance that criminals will succeed in breaking into a bank's central computers to steal funds. After all, this is a much more lucrative target than a single user's PC. But in most cases accountholders should not lose out – the bank would take the hit.

If a bank were to go bust because of such losses, current account customers and savers also have an industry safety net to fall back on to ensure they get at least some money back. The Financial Services Compensation Scheme guarantees the first £2,000 of any savings or current account balance with a bank, and 90 per cent of the next £33,000, up to a total maximum of £31,700. If you have a larger balance, sticking to a big name bank (or a bank with a big backer such as Egg, which is owned by Prudential) might be wise. Were there to be largescale online fraud against one of the new internet banks such as IF, Egg or Smile, the hope and expectation would be that the parent bank – if it had sufficient funds – would step in to cover the losses. Alternatively, consider spreading your funds across a number of banks.

On a smaller scale, if a criminal does misuse your account, you are also protected. NatWest, HSBC, Lloyds TSB and Barclays all offer full protection to users for losses if their account is hacked. Some banks take a slightly harder line: Smile, for example, expects customers to pay the first £50 themselves. But at all banks, protection will not apply if a customer is negligent or takes part in criminal activity, which is why it is so important to protect personal information.

Technology

When bank websites first launched in the late 1990s they were notoriously unreliable – some actually crashing at launch. Online banking systems have improved considerably since then, and most banks' systems will now work with most computer operating systems, including Apple Macs and both Netscape and Internet Explorer browsers. There are exceptions, though. Users of older operating systems, such as Windows 3.1, can encounter difficulties.

Internet banking is quite a demanding application for a computer and there are glitches, even with 'compatible' systems. Using the bank's demonstration website is a good way to test compatibility, but occasionally systems do not work quite as they should. In these circumstances, it's essential that the bank has a telephone helpdesk to fall back on.

Moneyfacts (www.moneyfacts.co.uk) and **Blay's Guides** (www.blays. co.uk), suppliers of best-buy tables to newspapers and other media, both have listings of accounts by interest rates. These are a good place to start to find best-paying accounts and compare them with what you have. Alternatively, websites like FT Your Money will have similar listings and account-finder tools.

Main banks and savings organisations

Here are the main banks and savings organisations:

Abbey National (www.abbeynational.co.uk)
Abbey National has made much of the higher-than-average interest rates on its current account, although the rates are the same whether you bank online or through a branch. On the internet, Abbey provides all the standard services, such as bill payment, funds transfer and statement browsing, as well as the ability to apply for or extend an overdraft. Some Abbey mortgage borrowers can see their mortgage account online, depending on the type of loan. Abbey National also offers an online-only savings account, e-saver, with better rates than in branches.

Your key to a high savings rate.

We have an account you can access quickly, from anywhere, anytime, day or night. An account that's totally flexible. An account that gives total control and competitive rates. An account called Direct Saver.

- You can apply and operate your account online.

- You can make deposits into your Direct Saver account from any UK bank or building society account you hold. So you can save what you want, when you want.

- You can also transfer money from your Direct Saver account into any UK bank or building society account giving you the flexibility you need.

Make it happen.

Start saving now.
Visit the Direct Saver site at
www.rbs.co.uk/2

The Royal Bank of Scotland

Award Winning Online Services

- Winner of the Mortgage Finance Gazette 2001 Innovator of the Year Award

- Winner of the Financial Sector Technology Awards 'Best use of New Media in Customer Facing Environments'

- Easy to use, high interest savings account

- Term assurance quote and buy facility

- Insurance quote and buy

Barclays (www.barclays.co.uk)

Barclays lays claim to being the UK's biggest online bank. It certainly offers all the main features users would expect, including setting up bill payments in advance, transfers between accounts and balances for both savings and current accounts from a single screen. Usefully, Barclays customers who also have a Barclaycard can pay their bills on the due date over the internet – paying from another bank takes four working days.

Alliance & Leicester (www.alliance-leicester.co.uk)

The former building society runs a fairly limited online banking service. Customers can view balances and transactions and order copy statements and foreign currency or travellers' cheques; but bill payments and fund transfers are limited to 'mandated' accounts, those that have been set up in advance, which might be restrictive for some users.

Bank of Scotland (www.bankofscotland.co.uk)

Bank of Scotland is now, with Halifax, part of the giant HBoS group. South of the border, BoS is concentrating on small business accounts, although its internet personal banking is available UK-wide. The service supports bill payments and a secure channel for sending messages to the bank – something more banks should offer.

Bristol & West (www.bristolandwestonline.co.uk)

Bristol & West does not offer a current account – just savings and investments – but customers can view their entire portfolios through the website. Bristol & West has a reasonable track record on 'direct' savings accounts, and although its rates are often beaten by online-only banks, some customers might prefer the reassurance that there are branches too. Overall, its service is clear and easy to use.

Cahoot (www.cahoot.com)

Cahoot is the online banking arm of Abbey National. Cahoot offers a current account, savings, credit cards, online share dealing and loans, all accessed via the website. Technically advanced, Cahoot supports internet, mobile access via Wap and interactive TV. Its rates are generally very good; the downside is that phone banking support is limited, but customers can use Abbey National cash machines.

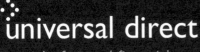
universal direct
straight forward financial products

a site for sore eyes

Tired of searching for the right mortgages and investments?
www.universal-direct.co.uk

Citibank (www.citibank.com/uk)

The UK arm of the US financial giant Citicorp was one of the first banks to offer a full online service, and it had a long track record in PC banking before that. The result is one of the most comprehensive online banking services on offer, with support for multi-currency accounts and international fund transfers to other Citibank accounts, as well as day-to-day services. The downsides are that Citibank has strict income criteria for new accounts, and other banks offer better interest rates.

Co-operative Bank (www.co-operativebank.co.uk)

The Co-operative Bank was one of the early adopters of online banking, but its systems are now showing their age a little: users have reported problems with newer browser software. These technical problems will pass, and the bank does offer some useful services, such as managing current accounts and credit cards from the same screen. The Co-op's Business Direct service is popular with small firms; the company also operates the popular internet bank Smile (see below).

Egg (www.egg.com)

Egg styles itself as an online bank but oddly offers no current account. What it does offer is a competitive savings account, operated totally over the internet. Accounts with phone and postal access pay less well. Egg guarantees that internet-only savings rates will match Bank of England base rates until 2007 – which is an attractive guarantee given the rate games banks and building societies usually play.

First Direct (www.firstdirect.co.uk)

HSBC-owned First Direct provides a comprehensive online banking service covering its current account and most of its other services. Users can see their credit card, savings and cash Isa, as well as current account balances from the welcome screen, and make money transfers and set up bill payments. First Direct will also send alerts to mobile phones when your salary arrives in your account, for example, or whenever there is a credit or debit.

Halifax (www.halifax.co.uk)
Former building society Halifax pays better interest rates than most banks on its current account, and supports this with full online banking. To qualify for the best interest rates, however, customers have to pay at least £1,000 a month into their current accounts. For Windows PC users, Halifax provides free anti-virus software and virus updates.

HSBC (www.hsbc.co.uk)
HSBC offers both internet and interactive TV banking. On the internet, users can amend standing orders, cancel direct debits and set up bill payments up to 12 months ahead, as well as download statement information for use in personal finance software packages.

Intelligent Finance (IF) (www.if.com)
A phone/internet arm of HBoS, Intelligent Finance pays better rates of interest on its current account than either Bank of Scotland or Halifax. As well as competitive in-credit interest, overdraft charges are low. There are no penalties, such as lower interest rates, for dealing with IF by phone.

Lloyds TSB (www.lloydstsb.co.uk)
Lloyds TSB provides internet access with all the usual features for its Select, Premier and Gold Service current accounts. This includes statement browsing, money transfers and bill payments, as well as the option of a linked internet savings account. Insomniacs, though, should look elsewhere: the Lloyds TSB service shuts between midnight and 4am.

National Savings (www.nationalsavings.co.uk)
The website of the government savings arm, whose unique products include Premium Bonds, tax-free Savings Certificates and Children's Bonus Bonds. The website includes a Savings Calculator that shows potential investment returns and an Unpaid Prize Finder for premium bond prizes.

Nationwide Building Society (www.nationwide.co.uk)

Although a building society, Nationwide is a strong player in the current account market and was one of the earliest operators to provide online banking, launching in 1997. The service has recently been revamped to provide a better interface and access from one screen to current accounts, e-savings, credit cards and mortgages.

NatWest (www.natwest.com)

NatWest provides its own, subscription-free internet service NatWest OnLine and free e-mails, both useful for newcomers to the internet. The bank offers full access to its current account and up to 20 accounts, including transaction details for the last six months. Investors can make use of online access to NatWest Stockbrokers too.

Norwich & Peterborough Building Society (www.npbs.co.uk)

Mutual building society Norwich & Peterborough is small compared to other online banks, but it still offers a full internet service through its Gold current account.

Royal Bank of Scotland (RBS) (www.rbs.co.uk)

RBS styles its online service 'digital banking', and it supports current accounts and most RBS-issued credit cards. As well as statement browsing, bill payments and transfers, its service is compatible with Microsoft Money and Quicken personal finance software.

Smile (www.smile.co.uk)

Smile is the internet arm of the Co-operative Bank, but it is quite a different proposition to its parent. Smile's accounts pay high interest rates, but there have been tales of people with otherwise unblemished financial records being turned down for a Smile current account. It's hard to say how much truth there is behind the rumours, but if Smile does let you have an account, it has one of the best deals out there.

Zurich Bank (www.zurichbank.co.uk)

Better known for insurance than for banking, Zurich offers a current account with an interest rate guarantee: rates will not be less than 0.5 per cent below Bank of England base rates. There are no branches but full internet access supports up to six sub-accounts per customer, as well as share portfolio tracking.

Building societies

Building societies continue to be worth considering for savings, with many societies particularly competitive on cash Isas. Windfalls are another key reason for not writing off these mutuals. With more than 60 building societies still around but many of them too small to remain competitive, it is a question of when – not if – more demutualise.

One recent study questioned whether most societies could afford the set-up costs of an internet savings service. However most societies do have at least informational websites – giving details of accounts, rates and how to contact the society.

Societies of course insist that they will not demutualise and that by remaining mutuals they can pay better rates to savers. To the degree that they do offer improved rates – and the real picture is very mixed – savers (and borrowers) are in a win-win position: better rates now, with the possibility of a windfall in the future.

Most societies require new savers to sign away their rights to any windfall for the first five years or more. However many will take that long to demutualise; equally, these rules may well be challenged legally. www.carpetbagger.com www.themoneybag.com and www.ordreport.co.uk are websites set up by windfall-seeking activists. They are the best places to pick up the latest news, advice and speculation on windfalls and demutualisation.

Barnsley Building Society
Permanent Building
Regent Street
Barnsley
South Yorkshire
S70 2EH
Tel: 01226 733 999
www.barnsley-bs.co.uk

Bath Investment & Building Society
20 Charles Street
Bath
Avon
BA1 1HY
Tel: 01225 423 271
www.bibs.co.uk

Beverley Building Society
57 Market Place
Beverley
East Yorkshire
HU17 8AA
Tel: 01482 881 510
www.beverleybs.co.uk

Britannia Building Society
Britannia House
Cheadle Road
Leek
Staffordshire
ST13 5RG
Tel: 01538 399 399
www.britannia.co.uk

Buckinghamshire Building Society
High Street
Chalfont St Giles
Buckinghamshire
HP8 4QB
Tel: 01494 879 500
www.bucksbuildingsociety.co.uk

Cambridge Building Society
PO Box 232
51 Newmarket Road
Cambridge
CB5 8FF
Tel: 01223 727 727
www.cambridge-building-society.co.uk

Catholic Building Society
7 Strutton Ground
Westminster
London
SW1P 2HY
Tel: 020 7222 6736
www.catholicbs.co.uk

Century Building Society
21–23 Albany Street
Edinburgh
Scotland
EH1 3QW
www.century-building-society.co.uk

Chelsea Building Society
Thirlestaine Hall
Thirlestaine Road
Cheltenham
Gloucestershire
GL53 7AL
Tel: 01242 271 271
www.thechelsea.co.uk

Chesham Building Society
12 Market Square
Chesham
Buckinghamshire
HP5 1ER
Tel: 01494 782 575
www.cheshambsoc.co.uk

Cheshire Building Society
Castle Street
Macclesfield
Cheshire
SK11 6AF
Tel: 01625 613 612
www.thecheshire.co.uk

Chorley & District Building Society
Key House
Foxhole Rd
Chorley
Lancashire
PR7 1NZ
Tel: 01257 279 373
www.chorleybs.co.uk

Clay Cross Building Society
Eyre Street
Clay Cross
Chesterfield
Derbyshire
S45 9NS
Tel: 01246 862 120
www.claycrossbs.co.uk

Coventry Building Society
Economic House
PO Box 9
High Street
Coventry
CV1 5QN
Tel: 0845 766 5522
www.coventrybuildingsociety.co.uk

Cumberland Building Society
Cumberland House
Castle Street
Carlisle
Cumbria
CA3 8RX
Tel: 01228 541 341
www.cumberland.co.uk

Darlington Building Society
Sentinel House
Lingfield Way
Darlington
Co Durham
DL1 4PR
Tel: 01325 366 366
www.darlington.co.uk

Derbyshire Building Society
PO Box 1
Duffield Hall
Duffield
Derby
DE56 1AG
Tel: 01332 841 000
www.thederbyshire.co.uk

Dudley Building Society
Dudley House
Stone Street
Dudley
West Midlands
DY1 1NP
Tel: 01384 231 414
www.dudleybuildingsociety.co.uk

Dunfermline Building Society
Caledonia House
Carnegie Avenue
Dunfermline
Fife
KY11 5PJ
Tel: 01383 627 727
www.dunfermline-bs.co.uk

Earl Shilton Building Society
22 The Hollow
Earl Shilton
Leicester
LE9 7NB
Tel: 01455 844 422
www.esbs.co.uk

Ecology Building Society
18 Station Road
Cross Hills
Near Keighley
West Yorkshire
BD20 7EH
Tel: 01535 635 933
www.ecology.co.uk

Furness Building Society
51–55 Duke Street
Barrow-in-Furness
Cumbria
LA14 1RT
Tel: 01229 824 560
www.furnessbs.co.uk

Hanley Economic Building Society
Granville House
Festival Park
Hanley
Stoke-on-Trent
Staffordshire
ST1 5TB
Tel: 01782 255 000
www.thehanley.co.uk

Harpenden Building Society
14–16 Station Road
Harpenden
Hertfordshire
AL5 4SE
Tel: 01582 765 411
www.harpendenbs.co.uk

Hinckley and Rugby Building Society
Upper Bond Street
Hinckley
Leicestershire
LE10 1DG
Tel: 01455 251 234
www.hrbs.co.uk

Holmesdale Building Society
43 Church Street
Reigate
Surrey
RH2 0AE
Tel: 01737 245 716
www.holmesdale.org.uk

Ipswich Building Society
44 Upper Brook Street
Ipswich
Suffolk
IP4 1DP
Tel: 01473 211 021
www.ipswich-bs.co.uk

Kent Reliance Building Society
Reliance House
Manor Road
Chatham
Kent
ME4 6AF
Tel: 01634 848 944
www.krbs.co.uk

Lambeth Building Society
118–120 Westminster Bridge Road
London
SE1 7XE
Tel: 020 7928 1331
www.lambeth.co.uk

Leeds & Holbeck Building Society
105 Albion Street
Leeds
West Yorkshire
LS1 5AS
Tel: 0113 225 7777
www.leeds-holbeck.co.uk

Leek United Building Society
50 St Edward Street
Leek
Staffordshire
ST13 5DH
Tel: 01538 384 151
www.leekunited.co.uk

Loughborough Building Society
6 High Street
Loughborough
Leicestershire
LE11 2QB
Tel: 01509 610 707
www.theloughborough.co.uk

Manchester Building Society
Manchester House
Queens Court
24 Queen Street
Manchester
M2 5AH
Tel: 0161 833 8888
www.themanchester.co.uk

Mansfield Building Society
Regent House
Regent Street
Mansfield
Nottinghamshire
NG18 1SS
Tel: 01623 676 300
www.mansfieldbs.co.uk

Market Harborough Building Society
Welland House
The Square
Market Harborough
Leicestershire
LE16 7PD
Tel: 01858 463 244
www.mhbs.co.uk

Marsden Building Society
6–20 Russell Street
Nelson
Lancashire
BB9 7NJ
Tel: 01282 440 500
www.marsdenbs.co.uk

Melton Mowbray Building Society
39 Nottingham Street
Melton Mowbray
Leicestershire
LE13 1NR
Tel: 01664 563 937
www.mmbs.co.uk

Mercantile Building Society
Mercantile House
The Silverlink Business Park
Wallsend
Tyne & Wear
NE28 9NY
Tel: 0191 295 9500
www.mercantile-bs.co.uk

Monmouthshire Building Society
Monmouthshire House
John Frost Square
Newport
South Wales
NP20 1PX
Tel: 01633 844 444
www.monbsoc.co.uk

National Counties Building Society
30 Church Street
Epsom
Surrey
KT17 4NL
Tel: 01372 742 211
www.ncbs.co.uk

Nationwide Building Society
Nationwide House
Pipers Way
Swindon
SN38 1NW
Tel: 01793 573 573
www.nationwide.co.uk

Newbury Building Society
17 Bartholomew Street
Newbury
Berkshire
RG14 5LY
Tel: 01635 555 700
www.newbury.co.uk

Newcastle Building Society
Portland House
New Bridge Street
Newcastle Upon Tyne
NE1 8AL
Tel: 0191 244 2000
www.newcastle.co.uk

Norwich & Peterborough Building Society
Peterborough Business Park
Lynch Wood
Peterborough
PE2 6WZ
Tel: 01733 372 372
www.npbs.co.uk

Nottingham Building Society
Nottingham House
5–13 Upper Parliament Street
Nottingham
NG1 2BX
Tel: 0115 948 1444
www.thenottingham.com

Portman Building Society
Portman House
Richmond Hill
Bournemouth
Dorset
BH2 6EP
Tel: 01202 292 444
www.portman.co.uk

Principality Building Society
PO Box 89
Principality Buildings
Queen Street
Cardiff
CF10 1UA
Tel: 029 2038 2000
www.principality.co.uk

Progressive Building Society
Progressive House
33–37 Wellington Place
Belfast
BT1 6HH
Tel: 028 9024 4926
www.theprogressive.com

Saffron Walden Herts & Essex Building Society
Saffron House
1a Market Street
Saffron Walden
Essex
CB10 1HX
Tel: 01799 522 211
www.swhebs.co.uk

Scarborough Building Society
Prospect House
PO Box 6
Scarborough
North Yorkshire
YO12 6EQ
Tel: 01723 368 155
www.scarboroughbs.co.uk

Scottish Building Society
23 Manor Place
Edinburgh
EH3 7XE
Tel: 0131 220 1111
www.scottishbldgsoc.co.uk

Shepshed Building Society
Bull Ring
Shepshed
Loughborough
Leicestershire
LE12 9QD
Tel: 01509 822 000
www.theshepshed.co.uk

Skipton Building Society
The Bailey
Skipton
North Yorkshire
BD23 1DN
Tel: 01756 705 000
www.skipton.co.uk

Stafford Railway Building Society
4 Market Square
Stafford
ST16 2JH
Tel: 01785 223 212
www.srbs.co.uk

Staffordshire Building Society
Jubilee House
PO Box 66
84 Salop Street
Wolverhampton
WV3 0SA
Tel: 01902 317 317
www.staffordshirebuildingsociety.co.uk

Stroud & Swindon Building Society
Rowcroft
Stroud
Gloucestershire
GL5 3BG
Tel: 01453 757 011
www.stroudandswindon.co.uk

Swansea Building Society
11 Cradock Street
Swansea
West Glamorgan
SA1 3EW
Tel: 01792 483 700
www.swansea-bs.co.uk

Teachers' Building Society
Allenview House
Hanham Road
Wimborne Minster
Dorset
BH21 1AG
Tel: 01202 843 500
www.teachersbs.co.uk

Tipton & Coseley Building Society
70 Owen Street
Tipton
West Midlands
DY4 8HG
Tel: 0121 557 2551
www.tipton-coseley.co.uk

Universal Building Society
Universal House
Kings Manor
Newcastle Upon Tyne
NE1 6PA
Tel: 0191 232 0973
www.theuniversal.co.uk

Vernon Building Society
19 St Petersgate
Stockport
Cheshire
SK1 1HF
Tel: 0161 429 6262
www.thevernon.co.uk

West Bromwich Building Society
374 High Street
West Bromwich
West Midlands
B70 8LR
Tel: 0121 525 7070
www.westbrom.co.uk

Yorkshire Building Society
Yorkshire House
Yorkshire Drive
Bradford
West Yorkshire
BD5 8LJ
Tel: 01274 740 740
www.ybs.co.uk

4

Sharedealing

The internet has transformed the world of stockmarket investment. The heady days of the internet boom and giving up your job to 'daytrade' shares to make your fortune may have gone. While some people made a lot of money, others lost more when the technology share bubble burst. However, the underlying investment technology that helped attract those previous novices to investing in the first place remains.

The internet has helped level the playing field for private investors with their counterparts in the City by giving access to up-to-the-minute prices, news and research as well as instant dealing – all at low cost.

Investors can now sit at home – or in the office – and trade through their computer screens without ever having to speak to a stockbroker. They can study share price graphs, see updated valuations of their portfolios, and place orders to buy or sell shares when they hit certain prices. And they can do all this for the lowest ever dealing commissions: online sharedealing has been one of the most competitive areas of internet finance, with free dealing promotions and flat-rate ongoing commissions as low as £10 a trade. A huge amount of research – whether charts of share prices or stockbroker analysis – is available for free on the web, often as part of dealing or portfolio monitoring services.

The internet and online dealing have certainly increased the number of active stockmarket investors. More than 10 million Britons hold shares, but traditionally the number of those who would have described themselves as investors was less than a million. There are said to be 300,000+ online share investors and at least some of these will either be new to investing or much more active than previously.

"You want to
deal online?"

zIf you want to deal online and take control of your investments, 24 hours a day, you need Brokerline Direct.com

BrokerlineDirect.com is a modern, efficient full nominee service that lets you get real time share quotations, review your portfolio and buy and sell shares online.

So, if you're looking to deal online you need to be looking at **www.brokerlinedirect.com**

For more information call us now on

01733 372237

or e-mail us at
info@npss.co.uk
(please quote reference DE1).

**Norwich and
Peterborough**
SHAREDEALING SERVICES

Industry research supports the view that online investors do trade more often than their offline counterparts, underlining how user-friendly many dealing services are but also how dangerously addictive the technology can be. Low dealing commissions mean even small investments of just a few hundred pounds can be practical; equally too much trading is a classic way of losing money in the stockmarket.

Dozens of online dealing services were launched in the internet boom time of 1999 and early 2000. In those days service was the big issue – could you deal when you wanted to or would the website crash on you? More recently, poor stockmarkets have led to falling sharedealing volumes. This, combined with the cut-throat pricing in the industry, has led to takeovers and other consolidation.

Tips for choosing an online sharedealing service

While investors should still look to keep a couple of dealing accounts to ensure they can always get access to the market, they also need to consider what would happen if a broker went out of business. In theory investors' shares should be automatically ring-fenced from a firm's financial problems. There is also the industry's Financial Services Compensation Scheme (FSCS) that guarantees to cover losses up to £48,000 (calculated as all of the first £30,000 and 90 per cent of the next £20,000). But cash is not covered by the FSCS.

With any dealing service they use or plan to use, investors should find out whether the broker has other insurance in place – many do, particularly the bigger firms. Dealing firms should be happy to give details.

Finally, online dealing services are almost exclusively execution-only – meaning you get no advice. That could change in the future, particularly with broadband allowing videoconferencing.

Price isn't everything. With dealing costs generally low, it is worth considering what else you might want – or what else is on offer – when choosing a broker. Services can vary a lot. Some points to consider are:

Investing online . . .

. . . the iShares answer

Investing online is all about buying what you want when you want to buy it, almost like the professionals do. Unfortunately, professional-style trading is not always matched by professional-style investment strategies. iShares, a new type of investment tool already big in the US, provides a solution.

Investment professionals (quite rightly) harp on about diversification or not putting all of your eggs in one basket. But at around £10 a trade plus stamp duty, many private investors choose just a handful of stocks to avoid trading costs and the hassle of researching a wide range of companies.

iShares offer an alternative. They are a type of fund, which can be bought just as you would an ordinary stock (a share costs about £5). But instead of being exposed to a single company you are buying exposure to an entire index of stocks. There is no stamp duty to pay either.

iShares already on the market track the FTSE 100, the FTSE TMT Index, the FTSE Euro 100 Index plus a whole range of European sector indices covering things like pharmaceutical and telecom stocks.

Because they trade like ordinary shares any time the market is open, they offer the flexibility that online investors crave. If you think that a particular piece of news or event is going to change the outlook for an industry, you can gain exposure to that industry rapidly by buying the appropriate iShares product – the iBloomberg Telecoms for instance.

In the past, you would have had to buy a few telecoms stocks and hoped that there would be no company-specific news that would undermine your investment decision. iBloomberg Telecoms, on the other hand, contains over 30 European telecoms stocks, offering truly diversified exposure.

iShares are flexible in a different way too. They can be bought as long-term investments, similar to a normal unit trust. With annual management fees as low as 0.35% they are very competitive. Online companies like comdirect offer iShares as part of an ISA or an existing PEP.

The case for tracking an index has been well made. Many active fund managers fail to beat the index on a regular basis, and for those that do, the investor will have to hand back much of that outperformance in terms of management fees. The buy-and-hold nature of index funds also avoids the trading costs that active fund managers incur every time they change their strategy.

We see iShares as the ultimate portfolio building block. Individuals can place their core investments in a lower-risk iShares tracker like the iFTSE-100, whilst making more speculative investments in sectors (and even individual stocks) with money that they are less worried about. Again this is a principle that many professional investors use – they call it "core-satellite" investing.

As individuals find their lives changing, the flexible nature of iShares allows the core-satellite balance to be tweaked, without the prohibitive entry and exit charges that some unit and investment trusts charge.

iShares is a product specifically designed to allow individuals to invest cheaply and efficiently, backed by the principles of diversification and risk control. If you would like to find out more, please visit www.ishares.net.

want a really flexible sector investment.

i|Shares™

The way you invest now. Only better.

For an investment that lets you diversify across all sectors, ask your stockbroker about iShares. Choose from the full range, stretching from Cyclicals, Financials, Industrials and Pharmaceuticals to Resources, Staples, Technology and Telecoms. For more information, visit our website or call us now.

ISAable PEPable SIPPable

0845 357 7000
www.ishares.net

- Are you just looking to trade in shares, or will you want to invest in funds, bonds, options or even more esoteric investment products such as spread-bets or Contracts For Difference (CFDs)?
- Do you want access to foreign stockmarkets?
- How much research do you want to be able to get from the broker's website, or are you happy to do your own?
- Do you need live prices and news, or are you prepared to accept a delay of say 15 minutes?
- Do you want limit orders, allowing shares to be bought and sold automatically when they hit chosen target prices?
- Do you want to be able to deal over the phone?
- Are you happy for your investments to be held electronically by the broker in a nominee account, rather than you being given a share certificate?
- What insurance or other compensation arrangements are there in case the broker gets into financial difficulties or your account is accessed fraudulently?
- How often are you likely to deal? Low dealing costs will be more important to investors who buy and sell frequently.
- What charges are there for transferring holdings away from the broker? If you are unhappy with the service or a better deal comes along you may want to switch.
- Do you want to buy shares in tax-free Isa form?
- Are you happy not to have advice and to deal on a so-called execution-only basis?
- What phone and e-mail support does the broker offer?

In addition, the website of the FSA (the Financial Services Authority, the chief investment watchdog) offers the following tips for online investors:

- Check the firm is legal. Unless an exemption applies, firms dealing in investment business with UK investors must be authorised by law, otherwise they are committing a criminal offence. Phone the FSA Consumer Helpline on 0845 606 1234 to check that the firm is authorised.

- If the firm isn't authorised, you won't be able to claim a single penny from the Investors Compensation Scheme if the firm goes bust and you've been badly advised, or the money you gave the firm is missing.

- Firms operating from European Union countries may also be able to do investment business lawfully in the UK and the FSA Consumer Helpline can check this out for you as well.

- If you buy shares or other investments from a firm based in another country you need to bear in mind the difficulty and expense of pursuing complaints – especially if the firm is unregulated. Different states have different laws so your rights will differ from country to country if the firm goes broke.

- A website with an address including .co.uk or just .uk doesn't always mean it's based in the UK. If you send your money to an illegal operator outside the jurisdiction of the UK courts, the chances of recovering any of your investment are close to zero.

- Don't be taken in by the look of the website. It may appear impressive but the cyber-cheats running it won't have the financial resources to back their scheme. More than likely, your cash will disappear down a black hole in cyberspace.

- Is the website you're visiting really the site you want? Is the address genuine? Sites run by legitimate firms can easily be copied. The address might be very similar to one used by a well-known company. If in doubt, look up the firm's number in the phone book and call them in person to double-check the site address. Don't rely on any phone number given on the website – this could be bogus too.

NB Even if a firm claims to be authorised, it's up to you to double-check whether it actually is. Don't just take the firm's word for it.

Blue Sky Ratings (www.blueskyratings.com)

This is a service that rates online stockbrokers across Europe. Ratings are based not just on the features a service offers but also the user-friendliness of the website. Blue Sky even tests customer service by checking e-mail and phone response times. Being able to get through on the phone to deal can be important when a site crashes or isn't working. 'Sods' Law' says this will coincide with a price crash or excessive volatility – when you most want to get in or out.

Blue Sky says it ignores price in its ratings, which some might see as unhelpful. True, investors can be too easily won over by low dealing prices rather than service or features. However, in reality price should and will be more or less important depending on how often you deal.

In Blue Sky's last update (dated October 2001) the most highly-rated brokers in the UK were (best first): Nothing Ventured; Schwab; Merrill Lynch HSBC; Comdirect; E*Trade; DLJ Direct; and Self Trade.

FT Your Money has a useful tool for helping investors find the best online stockbroker for their needs at http://ftyourmoney.ft.com/FTym/ brokerfinder – more than 100 different services are compared.

Money Supermarket (www.moneysupermarket.com) also has a price comparison tool.

The Association of Private Client Investment Managers & Stockbrokers (Apcims) at www.apcims.co.uk also has a search tool to find a stockbroker.

Investors Chronicle (www.investorschronicle.co.uk) has a wide variety of information on online stockbrokers. It also publishes an annual survey, which compares charges and gives awards based on reader research.

Stockbrokers' web addresses

American Express Sharepeople	www.sharepeople.com
Barclays Stockbrokers	www.barclays-stockbrokers.co.uk
Charles Schwab Europe	www.schwab-europe.com
Comdirect	www.comdirect.co.uk

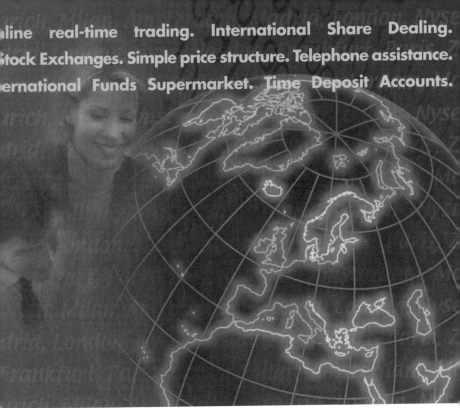

line real-time trading. International Share Dealing. Stock Exchanges. Simple price structure. Telephone assistance. ernational Funds Supermarket. Time Deposit Accounts.

Cortal's online brokerage service offers you direct online and telephone trading on London, Nyse, Nasdaq, Frankfurt, Paris, Zurich, Milan, Amsterdam and Madrid. With just one account and a simple price structure, you have less to worry about.

A world of investment opportunities awaits you.

Call us today **0800 169 0111** and quote ref. QF6 or visit **www.cortal.co.uk**

CORTAL Get more than your share
A company of BNP PARIBAS

DLJ Direct	www.dljdirect.co.uk
E-Cortal	www.e-cortal.com
E*Trade	www.etrade.co.uk
FasTrade	www.fastrade.co.uk
Fimatex	www.fimatex.co.uk
Halifax Sharedealing	www.sharexpress.co.uk
Hargreaves Lansdown	www.hargreaveslansdown.co.uk
IDealing	www.idealing.co.uk
IMIWeb	www.imiweb.co.uk
James Brearley & Sons	www.jbrearley.co.uk
Killik & Co	www.killik.co.uk
Merrill Lynch HSBC	www.mlhsbc.co.uk
My Broker	www.mybroker.com
Natwest Brokerline	www.natweststockbrokers.co.uk
Norwich Union Wealth Management	www.norwichunion.com
Nothing Ventured	www.nothing-ventured.com
Stocktrade	www.stocktrade.co.uk
TD Waterhouse	www.tdwaterhouse.co.uk

For what it's worth, the author has accounts with Comdirect and Selftrade. He has used Selftrade more, and prefers it.

Options, CFDs (Contracts For Difference), spread-betting

Cantor Index	www.cantorindex.co.uk
City Index	www.cityindex.co.uk
Deal4Free.com	www.deal4free.com
IG Index	www.igindex.co.uk

Investment research and shares information

London Stock Exchange (www.londonstockexchange.com)
Useful background and technical information, including on Techmark and Aim companies (respectively the UK's equivalent of Nasdaq, and the Alternative Investment Market for smaller, young firms).

Nasdaq (www.nasdaq.com)
The dotcom market. American, of course.

Teletext (www.teletext.co.uk)
As with the TV, has real-time share prices along with an online news service.

Proshare (www.proshare.co.uk)
Information on investment clubs and employee share ownership schemes.

The Financial Times (www.ft.com)
The FT stable offers a range of useful investor and stockmarket information and www.ft.com is the best starting point. It has links to FT Investor, Investors Chronicle magazine and CBS Marketwatch.

Bloomberg (www.bloomberg.co.uk)
Specialist City and investor news service.

Hemington Scott (www.hemscott.net)
Highly thought of research website (voted 'Best Research Provider' in the 2001 Investors Chronicle Investment Awards). Services include e-mail news alerts on companies you are interested in.

Citywire (www.citywire.co.uk)
Includes share tips from the City and directors' dealings.

Sharecast (www.sharecast.com)
Another news and research website owned by Durlacher Securities, a key dotcom stockbroker.

Both **Digital Look** (www.digitallook.com) and **Multex Investor** (www.multexinvestor.co.uk) have free company research from the City.

Breaking Views (www.breakingviews.com)
This offers stockmarket comment and opinions (for a fee). Set up by Hugo Dixon, former head of the Financial Times' Lex column and author of the clever, if difficult, *Penguin Guide to Finance*.

Ample Interactive Investor (www.ample.com)
Originally called Interactive Investor, known for having some of the liveliest bulletin boards/chatrooms.

ADVFN (Advanced Financial Network) (www.advfn.com)
Also known for its bulletin boards.

5

Isas and Investment Funds

The investment industry (and some politicians) have been talking for decades about Britons becoming a nation of shareholders. But even the sophisticated online sharedealing services now available have only succeeded in winning over at most a few hundred thousand investors – so far at least.

More than 10 million Britons may hold shares in individual companies, but in the vast majority of cases this is because they bought them in apparently no-lose privatisations or were given them in demutualisations or by their employers. Halifax (now HBoS) is still the most widely held share in the UK. Few of these shareholders have gone on to invest in more shares. When it comes to stockmarket investments they are more likely to have taken out a tax-free Isa (or Pep previously) whose underlying investment is a fund of shares, normally a unit trust.

The internet has a wealth of information on Isas and investment funds. Traditionally, investors have been sent fund valuations every six months or so; as with shares the internet offers them up-to-date prices and performance monitoring.

Online fund 'supermarkets' – so-called because they sell funds from different investment managers in a single Isa, allowing investors much wider choice – have also added to competitive pressures on prices, and made switching investments easier. Fund supermarkets already account for some quarter of all Isa sales and this figure should deservedly continue to grow.

Background information

Association of Unit Trusts and Investment Funds (www.investment-funds.org.uk) (020 7831 0898)

Website of the industry body that represents most Isa and investment companies. Has shortcuts to the different investment managers' websites; a range of free guides and factsheets on, for example, investing for children, Isas and ethical investment; and statistics on amounts of money invested in and taken out of funds.

Association of Investment Trust Companies (AITC)
(www.aitc.co.uk) (020 7282 5555)

Website of the investment trust trade association. It also has a range of factsheets, guidance and contact information.

Isa, unit trust and Oeic company websites

Abbey National	www.abbeynational.co.uk
Aberdeen Unit Trust Managers	www.aberdeen-asset.com
Aberforth Unit Trust Managers	www.aberforth.co.uk
ABN AMRO Fund Managers	www.abnamrofunds.co.uk
ACM Investments	www.acmfunds.com
AEGON Asset Management	www.abetterway.co.uk
Allchurches Investment Management	www.eigonline.com
Artemis Unit Trust Managers	www.artemisonline.co.uk
AXA Fund Managers	www.axa.co.uk
B&CE Unit Trust Management	www.bandce.co.uk
Baillie Gifford	www.bailliegifford.com
Barclays Funds	www.barclays.com
Baring Fund Managers	www.baring-asset.com
Britannic Asset Management	www.britannicasset.com
Britannic Unit Trust Managers	www.britannic.co.uk
BWD Rensburg Unit Trust Managers	www.bwd-rensburg-unit-trusts.co.uk

Our fund's 8.7% regular income is consistent so you can be all over the place

JPMF UK Corporate Bond Fund

The JPMorgan Fleming UK Corporate Bond Fund enables you to avoid the volatility of equities without missing out on high returns. Through a diverse portfolio of quality corporate bonds, our expert bond management team consistently achieves 8.7%,* compared to just 5.8%** from the average Building Society. You can choose to receive your returns as a regular income or reinvest them for long-term capital growth. So why not make the JPMF UK Corporate Bond Fund your next ISA? You'll be surprised how far it could take you.

For more information, contact your financial adviser, return the coupon below or call us free on **0800 20 40 20** quoting the reference below

www.jpmorganfleming.com

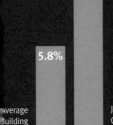

8.7%

5.8%

Average
Building
Society**

JPMF UK
Corporate
Bond Fund*

JPMorgan Fleming
Asset Management

Please send me details about the JPMF UK Corporate Bond Fund. Return to: JPMorgan Fleming Asset Management, FREEPOST, Romford, RM1 3XB.

Mr/Mrs/Miss   Initials   Surname   Address

Postcode   Telephone

REF 2921/004

JPMF UK Corporate Bond Fund

A high-income alternative to a building society account

JPMF UK Corporate Bond Fund has been specifically designed to meet the needs of investors frustrated by the low rates of interest on offer at banks and building societies.

The fund concentrates on the generation of income, offering a yield that beats most conventional savings accounts. Capital growth is a secondary consideration so this fund is designed for investors who are more keen to maximise income than to grow their original capital.

A Regular Income

JPMF UK Corporate Bonds Fund invests in a range of quality corporate bonds issued by UK companies and some overseas companies as well. The fund uses the yield these bonds pay to provide investors with a regular income, currently 8.2% (A) per annum. This compares very favourably to the 2.3 %(B) generated by the average Building Society 90-day notice account.

Flexibility and Freedom

JPMF UK Corporate Bond Fund is also highly flexible. You can choose to take a regular income, or instead you can let the income roll-up in the fund to increase the value of capital.

You can invest for as long as you wish – however, we recommend that you invest for at least five years in order to make the most of the opportunity for growth and overcome any short-term market volatility. When it's time to take your money out, there are no penalties to pay whatsoever.

Who is it Suitable For?

Investors who want to achieve a high income, first and foremost.

Our Proven Investment Process

Through careful analysis and research we look to reduce risk in our funds and improve investment performance. We use a disciplined investment process to determine the best shares and bonds to hold across our fund range. Our fund managers never hold a stock without following this process to the letter.

1 Rank each potential stock
We analyse each potential 'buy' in our investment universe using a combination of four performance predictors. Using these models, we have developed our own independent ranking system which allows us to rate each bond and share in our investment universe. These rankings are continuously reviewed so we can quickly identify a change in a stock's relative attractions.

2. Research the company
Once we have identified suitable investment opportunities, we analyse a company to assess its long-term attractions, looking at its market position, the quality of its management, its cash flow and its sales growth. On average, our investment teams visit 5,000 companies a year across the world to discuss their management strategies.

3. Look at the wider picture
Finally we examine how each company fits into the wider economic environment and our investment strategy for each fund. We assess factors such as interest rates, globalisation, technology and demographics, all of which have an impact on the markets and industry sectors we are investing in.

CONSTRUCTING OUR FUNDS

All of our funds are constructed within strict risk parameters. We are careful how much we invest in any single stock, sector or region and we constantly monitor the volatility within each fund. In this way, we aim to ensure that we are not simply delivering superior returns – but superior, risk-adjusted returns.

All figures sourced Standard & Poor's Micropal – www.micropal.com Figures as at 01.12.01, mid to mid, UK Sterling, PEP/ISA tax. (A) Current gross annual yield as at 01.12.01. (B) Represented by UK Savings 2500+ Gross Investment Index. Please note, the quoted yield is not guaranteed and may vary and any income you may receive may therefore also fluctuate. Past performance is not a guide to future returns. The value of investments and the income from them may go down as well as up, and you might get back less than you invested. Your capital in a Building society is secure, whereas in a stock market linked investment it is exposed to a certain degree of risk. The fund management charges will be deducted from the capital account. While this will boost the income and the quoted yield, it will also constrain capital growth.

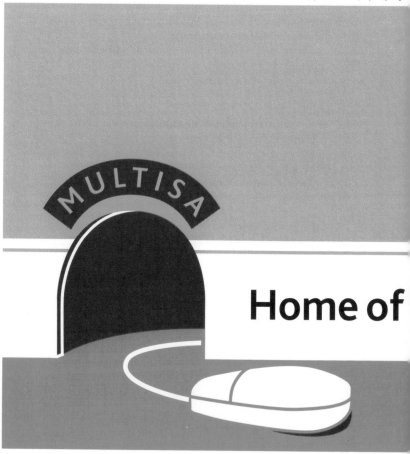

Home of

Skandia's range of over 240 funds from more than 20 world class fund groups is just a few clicks away - with 24-hour online services that include portfolio valuation. Skandia makes no annual charge in the first year of new accounts, nor any charge thereafter if the account value remains above £10,000, and switching is fast and cost effective.

the on-line ISA.

For details, visit www.skandia.co.uk/multifundshop or ask your IFA for details.

Skandia

The leader in multi-manager investment

E-mail, E-marketing, E-commerce

E-mail, E-marketing, E-commerce – just a load of E's or ZZZ's?

With more than 1 in 3 UK adults having access to the internet, the use of technology is now part of everyday life. Technology within the financial services sector is no exception, but is it exciting?

Every week in the press we are seeing the birth of new financial websites each striving to offer a new innovative approach to the market. Independent Financial Advisers (IFAs) now expect a variety of on-line services to be delivered either directly from insurance providers or via one of the financial services portals. IFAs' clients, in turn, have the same expectations from their adviser.

So what are the key benefits to the IFA from the services available?

To coin a much over-used phrase, access to information 24x7 is one of the greatest benefits the internet can offer. This can range from a simple download of an application form or checking the day's fund prices, to client specific information such as policy valuations. So, even if information is needed at the last minute, it's available at the click of a mouse.

The internet is also the most powerful research tool available, allowing IFAs and their clients to easily access information. This enables quicker comparisons to be made without the need to trawl through reams of paper, which often can be out of date.

Insurance providers can build their own centres of research within their websites for IFAs through generic industry information such as up-to-the-minute news articles, technical bulletins, Budget summaries, tax tables and so on. These educational tools can also benefit IFAs in training their own staff. Better trained staff = better advice for the client.

The use of on-line applications and fund switching ensure that instructions are

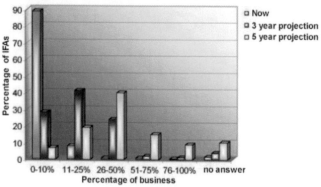

Source: Skandia Pathfinder Forum June 2001

carried out quickly with no errors, giving IFAs and their clients the opportunity to make timely decisions on transactions. Policies issued quicker will result in happier clients.

Isn't it surprising then that very few IFAs conduct more than 10% of their business on-line at the moment - but this is set to change over the next few years. It's therefore important that insurance companies understand how IFAs use on-line services and include them in the development process to create flexible and intuitive solutions to meet their needs. It is also important for IFAs to continually demonstrate added value over competitors – so the use of on-line tools is a must.

An increasing number of IFAs are starting to use insurance providers services to download information straight into their back office systems, removing the need for manual data input.

But it's not just insurance providers who offer internet-based services. Increasingly IFAs are recognising the importance of having their own website. In a survey conducted by Skandia in 2000 of a number of its IFAs, 85% had their own websites. Undoubtedly this figure will have increased into 2001 so IFAs without a site must ensure they do not get left behind in this fast-developing arena.

IFA websites vary greatly from a simple on-line business card to content rich sites offering services such as fund supermarkets and investment profiling tools. Clearly, developing a website incurs costs which can vary enormously. IFAs can choose to build their sites through web building packages, now widely available, or choose to employ a software developer to build a bespoke site. But the work does not stop once the site is built. Continually updating the site to ensure it's current and relevant are of equal, if not greater, importance.

IFAs must ensure their sites have that 'sticky factor' to generate interest and guarantee return visits from prospective and existing clients - after all nobody

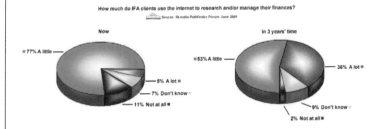

How much do IFA clients use the internet to research and/or manage their finances?
Source: Skandia Pathfinder Forum June 2001

Now

≡77% A little
5% A lot ≡
7% Don't know
11% Not at all ≡

In 3 years' time

≡53% A little
36% A lot ≡
9% Don't know
2% Not at all ≡

would want to read the same newspaper twice. One cost-efficient way of adding new content to IFAs websites can be simply achieved through hyperlinks to topical and relevant websites.

With a whole raft of information and services, ease of navigation and speed of downloading pages are key to keeping visitors within a website. If help is needed during a visit to a website then this too must be easy to get, either on-line or through more traditional routes.

Canada Life Management	www.canadalife.co.uk
Cazenove Investment Fund Management	www.cazenove.com
CIS Unit Managers	www.cis.co.uk
City Financial Managers	www.cityfinancial.co.uk
Clerical Medical Investment Funds	www.clericalmedical.co.uk
Close Fund Management	www.closefm.com
Credit Suisse Asset Management	www.csamfunds.co.uk
Deutsche Asset Management	www.deam-uk.co.uk/invest/
Direct Line Unit Trusts	www.directline.com
Dresdner RCM	www.dresdnerrcm.co.uk
Edinburgh Fund Managers	www.edfd.com
Exeter Investment Group	www.exeter.co.uk
F&C Management	www.fandc.co.uk
Fidelity Investments	www.fidelity.co.uk
First State Investments	www.firststate.co.uk
Framlington	www.framlington.co.uk
Franklin Templeton Investment Management	www.franklintempleton.co.uk
Friends Provident Unit Trust Managers	www.friendsprovident.co.uk
Gartmore Fund Managers	www.gartmore.com
Global Asset Management	www.gam.com
Govett Investment Management	www.govett.co.uk
Halifax Investment Fund Managers	www.halifaxequitable.co.uk
Halifax Unit Trust Management	www.halifax.co.uk
Henderson Global Investors	www.henderson.com
Hill Samuel Unit Trust Managers	www.swipartnership.co.uk
Homeowners Investment Fund Managers	www.homeowners.co.uk
Invesco Perpetual	www.invescoperpetual.co.uk
Investec Asset Management	www.investecfunds.co.uk
JP Morgan Fleming Asset Management	www.jpmorganfleming.com
Jupiter Unit Trusts	www.jupiterifa.co.uk

Lazard Fund Managers	www.lazardnet.com
Legal & General Unit Trust Managers	www.legalandgeneral.com
LeggMason Investors Asset Managers	www.leggmasoninvestors.com
Lincoln Unit Trust Managers	www.lutm.co.uk
Liontrust Asset Management	www.liontrust.co.uk
Lombard Odier Unit Trust Managers	www.lombardodier.com
M&G Group	www.mandg.co.uk
Manek Investment Management	www.manek.co.uk
Marks & Spencer Financial Services	www.marksandspencer.com/financialservices
Marlborough Fund Managers	www.marlboroughfunds.com
Martin Currie Unit Trusts	www.martincurrie.com
Merrill Lynch Investment Managers	www.mlim.co.uk
MGM Unit Managers	www.mgm-assurance.co.uk
Morley Investment Services	www.morleyfm.com
Murray Johnstone Unit Trust Management	www.murrayjohnstone.com
New Star Asset Management	www.newstaram.com
Newton Fund Managers	www.newton.co.uk
NFU Mutual Unit Managers	www.nfumutual.co.uk
NPI Investment Managers	www.npi.co.uk
Old Mutual Fund Managers	www.oldmutualfunds.co.uk
Pearl Unit Trusts	www.amp-pearl.co.uk
Premier Portfolio Managers	www.premierfunds.co.uk
Prudential Unit Trusts	www.pru.co.uk
Quilter Fund Management	www.quilterfundmanagement.co.uk
Rathbone Unit Trust Management	www.rathbones.com
Rothschild Asset Management	www.fivearrows.com
Royal & Sun Alliance Unit Trust Management	www.rsainvestments.com
Royal London Unit Trust Managers	www.royal-london.co.uk
Sanwa International Investment Services	www.sanwa-am.co.uk

Sarasin Investment Funds	www.sarasin.co.uk
Schroder Investments	www.schroders.com
Scottish Amicable Life	www.scottishamicable.co.uk
Scottish Friendly Asset Managers	www.scottishfriendly.co.uk
Scottish Life Investments	www.scottishlife.co.uk
Scottish Mutual Assurance	www.scottishmutual.co.uk
Scottish Widows Fund Management	www.scottishwidows.co.uk
SG Asset Management	www.sgam.co.uk
Singer & Friedlander Asset Management	www.sfim.co.uk
Skandia	www.skandia.co.uk
SLC Asset Management	www.slcam.co.uk
Smith & Williamson Unit Trust Managers	www.smith.williamson.co.uk
Sovereign Unit Trust Managers	wwww.teachers-group.co.uk
Standard Life Investments	www.standardlifeinvestments.co.uk/retail
Threadneedle Investments	www.threadneedle.co.uk
Tilney Collective Management	www.tilney.com
UBS Asset Management Unit Managers	www.phillipsdrew.com
Virgin Money Management Services	www.virginmoney.com
Wesleyan Assurance Society	www.wesleyan.co.uk
Woolwich Unit Trust Managers Limited	www.wutm.co.uk

Investment trust management groups

3i Investments	www.3i.com (020 7928 3131)
Aberdeen Asset Managers	www.aberdeen-asset.com (0500 000 040)
Aberforth Partners	www.aberforth.co.uk (0131 220 0733)

Amerindo Investment Advisors	www.amerindo.co.uk (020 7629 2349)
Asset Management Investment Company	www.amicplc.com (020 7329 1290)
Baillie Gifford & Co	www.bailliegifford.com (0800 027 0133)
Barclays Global Investors	www.barclaysglobal.com (020 7668 8661)
Baring Asset Management	www.baring-asset.com (020 7628 6000)
BFS Investments	www.bfsinvest.co.uk (01483 238 418)
Blue Planet Investment Management	www.blueplanet.ac (0131 226 6040)
Britannic Investment Managers	www.britannicasset.com (0141 222 8000)
Candover Investments	www.candover.com (020 7489 9848)
Close Finsbury Asset Management	www.closefinsbury.co.uk (0800 169 6968)
Close Fund Services	www.aisinvest.com (01481 710607)
Deutsche Investment Trust Managers	www.deam-uk.com/uk/invest (020 7545 0520)
Dresdner RCM Global Investors	www.dresdnerrcm-its.co.uk (020 7475 6151)
Dunedin Capital Partners	www.dunedin.com (0131 225 6699)
Edinburgh Fund Managers (EFM)	www.edfd.com (0800 028 6789)
Exeter Asset Management	www.exeter.co.uk (01392 253 225)
F&C Management	www.fandc.co.uk (020 7628 8000)

Fidelity Investments International	www.fidelity.co.uk (01732 361 144)
First State Investments	www.itssaints.co.uk (0131 473 2200)
Framlington Investment Management	www.framlington.co.uk (0845 777 5511)
Franklin Templeton Investment Management	www.franklintempleton.co.uk (0131 469 4000)
Friends Ivory & Sime	www.itszerocharge.co.uk (08457 99 22 99)
Gartmore Investment Management	www.gartmore.com (020 7782 2000)
Genesis Fund Managers	www.giml.co.uk (020 7201 7200)
Govett Investment Management	www.aibgovett.com (020 7378 7979)
Henderson Global Investors	www.henderson.com (0800 106 106)
Herald Investment Management	www.heralduk.com (020 7553 6300)
HG Capital	www.hgcapital.net (020 7203 5555)
Invesco Asset Management	www.invesco.co.uk/investment-trusts (020 7626 3434)
Investec Investment Management	www.investec.com (020 7597 1800)
J Rothschild Capital Management	www.ritcap.co.uk (0131 525 9819)
JP Morgan Fleming Asset Management	www.jpmorganfleming.co.uk/its (01708 776 851)
Jupiter Asset Management	www.jupiteronline.co.uk (020 7468 6469)
Kleinwort Capital	www.kleinwortcapital.com (020 7475 5021)

Law Debenture	www.lawdeb.co.uk
	(020 7606 5451)
Lazard Freres Asset Management	www.lazard.com
Legal & General Investment	www.legal-and-general.co.uk
Management	(020 7528 6883)
Leggmason Investors	www.leggmasoninvestors.com
	(020 7537 0000)
Liontrust Investment Services	www.liontrust.co.uk
	(020 7412 1766)
Majedie Investments	www.majedie.co.uk
	(020 7626 1243)
Martin Currie Asset Management	www.martincurrie.com/its
	(0131 229 5252)
Maunby Investment Management	www.maunby.demon.co.uk
	(01423 523 553)
Merrill Lynch Investment Managers	www.mlim.co.uk
	(0800 445 522)
Montanaro Investment Managers	www.montanaro.co.uk
	(01392 412 122)
Northern Venture Managers	www.nvm.co.uk
	(0800 028 6789)
Pictet Asset Management	www.pictect.com
	(020 7847 5000)
Polar Capital Partners	www.polarcapital.co.uk
	(020 7592 1500)
Progressive Asset Management	www.pro-asset.com
	(020 7490 4355)
Renaissance Capital Group	www.rencapital.com
Royal London Asset Management	www.rlam.co.uk
	(020 7818 6804)
Rutland Fund Management	www.rutlandtrust.com
	(020 7225 3391)
Schroder Investment Management	www.schroder.co.uk
	(020 7658 6000)

Scottish Investment Trust   www.sit.co.uk (0131 225 7781)
Scottish Value Management   www.scottish-value.co.uk
       (0131 226 7660)
Sloane Robinson Investment   www.sloanerobinson.com
       (020 7929 8810)

Fund supermarkets and discount brokers

Ample (www.ample.com) (0845 88 00 267)
Fund supermarket owned by Australian financial group AMP and which incorporates Interactive Investor website.
Features:

- sells 400+ Isa funds and unit trusts from 24 fund managers at a discount;
- includes true management cost figures (so-called Total Expense Ratios or TERs);
- buy online, advice and tips;
- also Portfolio Centre for monitoring investments including shares and pension funds, charting tools, latest investment news, stock alerts and broker forecasts.

Bestinvest (www.bestinvest.co.uk) (020 7321 0100)
Opinionated (and intelligent) discount investment broker.
Features:

- sells 700+ funds online from 41 management groups at a discount;
- useful free guides on personal pensions, 'dog' investment funds, with-profits bonds and others;
- news on manager and fund group changes and moves;
- tools and advice on tax planning, portfolio management and asset allocation;
- also discounts on with-profits bonds and Venture Capital Trusts (VCTs).

Charcol (www.charcolonline.co.uk) (0800 358 5559)
Fund supermarket owned by mortgage broker Charcol, now part of
Bradford & Bingley.
Features:

- sells around 400 Isa funds from 27 management companies at a
  discount;
- online fund adviser to help choose right investments;
- online financial healthcheck;
- information and advice about savings and investments;
- also online savings account, mortgages, pensions and insurance.

Egg Invest (www.egg.com) (0870 010 7400)
Fund supermarket owned by online bank Egg, which is owned by
Prudential.
Features:

- sells 260 Isa funds from 24 management firms at a discount;
- also sharedealing, online credit cards and statements, savings
  accounts, insurance and shopping.

Fidelity Funds Network (www.fundsnetwork.co.uk) (0800 41 41 61)
Fund supermarket owned by Fidelity, the US investment giant.
Features:

- sells 560 funds from 37 managers at a discount;
- awards include 'Best use of new media' – Money Marketing 2001;
  'Best fund provider website' – Investor's Week 2000.

Hargreaves Lansdown (www.hargreaveslansdown.co.uk) (0117 900
9000)
One of Britain's biggest independent financial adviser firms, Hargreaves
offers some of the best discounts around on investment funds and other

SUPERMARKET SWEEP
By Paul Stallard, Vice President, Marketing and Business Development

With fund supermarkets set to increase UK retail investment into collective schemes from £259 billion to £555 billion by 2004 , this year has seen many providers introducing fund supermarket services which offer increasing flexibility to investors.

With the launch of its own UK Fund Supermarket, TD Waterhouse's entry into this market is a reflection of the company's focus on customer care and service excellence. Listening to customer needs and working hard at all our products and services are a continuous process.

This dedication to providing service excellence has been recognised by our customers and reflected by our scooping the awards for Best Dealing Only Broker and Overall Stockbroker of the Year for 2001, by readers of the Investors Chronicle.

The concept of the fund supermarket is new to investors in the UK. The idea of providing retail investors with low cost, direct access to a wide variety of investment vehicles under one roof has been hugely successful in the US. Fund supermarkets now account for more than 10% of all fund distribution in the US and a similar impact is expected here in the UK .

The concept of the fund supermarket is as its name suggests. A company, such as TD Waterhouse, provides a diverse range of unit trust and OEIC products with varying levels of risk from different asset managers (Schroders, M&G, Invesco Perpetual etc). Using a variety of research tools provided, customers can calculate their required levels of risk and regional focus. They can then identify the funds with the best performance in that sector and of course, make the purchase.

A fund supermarket can aggregate all purchases made by customers and deal with the fund companies in bulk. This allows the fund supermarket owner to negotiate on costs, passing on considerable savings to customers.

For example, if someone is looking to invest £10,000 through the TD Waterhouse service (with an average discounted initial sales charge of 1.5%) the initial sales charge on the account is £150. If a traditional channel is used (with an average initial sales charge of 5.25%) a customer would pay around £525. Using a fund supermarket, in this case, results in a saving of £375.

As well as the low cost nature of fund supermarkets, they also provide an easy and convenient method for first time investors to get a foothold in the marketplace. A first time investor may not have enough capital to gain a wide enough spread of investments through individual equity holdings. This will ultimately prevent them from spreading their portfolio's risk broadly enough to weather any storms. However, investing in a collective investment scheme through a fund supermarket can spread the risk over hundreds of individual stocks.

In addition, collective investment schemes come midway on the risk scale between cash and the higher risk individual equity investment. With global markets in a state of flux, investors looking for exposure to markets may find that investing through a fund supermarket perfectly suits their requirements.

Figures from Autif (www.investmentfunds.org.uk/industry_data/ukfum/performance) and The Cerulli Report – Trends in the UK Retail Fund Marketplace.
Scotland on Sunday, 3rd June 2001.

WATERHOUSE

Professional investors also use fund supermarkets, as fund investment plays an important part of any portfolio's asset allocation. Not only do fund supermarkets allow investors the scope to look at sectors that may have a limited offering in the UK market such as the engineering and mining sectors, but it can also provide access to overseas shares.

With market sentiment in the UK remaining nervous at present, a wide range of opportunities across the rest of the world still remains. The UK market represents only 9.7% of the total capitalisation of the MSCI World Index, and investors who focus solely on the UK could be missing out on opportunities in the other 90% outside our borders. However, for a UK investor, gaining access to in depth knowledge of these opportunities isn't always possible. Following and investing in overseas stocks individually can be time consuming and expensive.

The TD Waterhouse Fund Supermarket provides investors with in-depth research on each fund – covering amongst other things performance summaries, manager profiles, top holdings and size of the funds. Investors can build up their knowledge of the market by following fund reports until they feel confident enough to branch out into individual shares.

Surprisingly for such an equity friendly country, the fund supermarket industry in the UK is only the fourth largest in Europe. However, it is the second fastest growing as investors increasingly recognise its value for all levels of investment strategy. By 2004 Cerulli associates predict that fund supermarkets will account for over 30% of UK retail fund sales.

So if you're nervous about investing at the moment or merely looking to adjust your portfolio holdings; use a fund supermarket to shop around and find the best deal.

TD WATERHOUSE'S FUND SUPERMARKET

TD Waterhouse's Fund Supermarket was launched in July 2001 and offers investors the choice of around 400 funds accessible via telephone and the web. Funds purchased can be consolidated into one account with any other shares and cash holdings, held in a regular trading account, or within an ISA wrapper. The service offers investors access to institutional fund research and analysis of market leading funds. The service aims to offer investors the broadest possible choice, ease of use and substantial savings. For further information, call 0845 607 6001 or log onto www.tdwaterhouse.co.uk and go to the Fund Supermarket section.

The value of investments and the income from them may fall as well as rise and you may not get back all that you have invested. If you are in any doubt as to the suitability of an investment you should seek advice from your usual financial adviser.

TD Waterhouse Investor Services (Europe) Ltd, a subsidiary of TD Waterhouse Group Inc. is a member of the London Stock Exchange and regulated by The FSA.

financial products – even paying annual loyalty bonuses to investors. Website offers a range of services including:

- daily news;
- details of discounts;
- portfolio tool;
- shareholder perks guide and registration for being sent other free guides;
- low-cost online sharedealing.

TD Waterhouse (www.tdwaterhouse.co.uk) (0845 607 6001)
Fund supermarket run by US investment giant of same name, relatively new in UK.
Features:

- sells 400 Isa funds from 20 management groups;
- explanations of investment jargon including fund management 'styles', asset allocation and diversification;
- stockmarket news;
- also comprehensive sharedealing service.

Torquil Clark (www.tqonline.co.uk) (0800 41 31 86)
Another online fund supermarket/discount broker. Offers discounts on 500+ Isa funds. It also has online guides, life insurance, pensions and stockbroking.

Wiseup (www.wiseup.com)
Online fund supermarket of IFA Bates Investment Services.
Features:

- buy online;
- auto advice service gives fund recommendations;
- online guide to Isas, and Isa FAQs (frequently asked questions).

Other discount brokers include **Chartwell** (www.chartwell-investment.co.uk), which has a range of useful free guides, and the **ISA Shop** (www.isa-shop.co.uk).

Chase de Vere Investments (www.chasedevere.co.uk) has useful guides and performance statistics, as well as saving rates.

Performance and research

'Past performance is no guide to the future' says the advertising small-print, a mantra backed up by research from the chief financial watchdog, the FSA. However, past performance remains the single most enticing way of advertising a fund. The web has plenty of performance data but some websites also offer other measures for attempting to pick the winners of the future.

Trustnet (www.trustnet.com) (020 7439 3160)
An excellent free site for checking and monitoring performance of investment funds, including personal pension and life insurance-linked funds. Earns its money from charging the fund management companies. It offers:

- daily price and performance data;
- fund information, including contact details and charges (including Total Expense Ratios or TERs), charts, including comparisons with stockmarkets;
- portfolio tool for online valuations. Trustnet will also send price and valuation e-mail alerts to investors;
- financial news;
- online guides to Isas, fund supermarkets, ethical investment, unit trusts and Oeics, Exchange Traded Funds, Split Capital investment trusts, and Venture Capital Trusts (VCTs);

- currency exchange rates;
- tool for helping choose an Isa.

FT Fund Ratings and **FT Investor services** (www.ft.com)
FT Fund Ratings assesses the level of risk of investment strategy, as well as charges and performance of funds underpinning Isas, pensions and Peps. FT Investor has fund news.

Citywire (www.citywire.co.uk)
A useful website, apparently aimed at investment advisers as well as savvy investors. In its Fund News section there is its own interesting performance rating of individual investment managers (rather than funds themselves), some well-thought-out fund recommendations and details of shares funds have been buying.

Other fund performance and rating services include **Standard & Poor's** (www.funds-sp.com), **Lipper** (www.lipperleaders.com), **Morningstar** (www.morningstar.co.uk), and **Riskmetrics** (www.riskgrades.com).

6

Credit Cards and Loans

Credit cards

The internet would not be where it is today without the credit card. In the UK, four out of five internet purchases are on a credit card, according to the research company Forrester. On most websites with something to sell, credit cards are the only way to pay.

Credit card fraud and protection

Often, though, using a credit card online is associated with fraud or, at least, the risk of fraud. The UK has one of the highest rates of credit card fraud anywhere in the world, and much of the blame – rightly or wrongly – is attributed to the growth in online shopping and e-commerce.

Losses through debit and credit card fraud were more than £400m in 2001, up 30 per cent on 2000's figures. Around a fifth of that figure was fraud carried out with stolen card details – by phone, mail order or the internet.

APACS, the industry body that manages card payments, does not publish exact figures for internet fraud. However, the organisation points out that fraud using the internet is relatively small, at least when it is set against the sums involved for mail order and phone losses.

But despite the concerns, the key point is that fraud is essentially a problem for card issuers rather than consumers. A customer's liability to fraudulent use of their card on- or offline is generally limited to £50 and some card companies guarantee no liability at all (see below). Internet fraud might be worrying and it might be a hassle to fill in forms to get a new card, but fundamentally it should cost you little – if anything.

The bigger risk is in dealing with dodgy retailers who fail to deliver. But – and this is a positive reason for using a credit card online – if your purchase is for more than £100, you may well be able to fall back on the card company for a refund if there are problems.

Even when internet fraud does happen, it is usually far more basic than some of the stories about the dangers of the internet suggest. There have been few, if any, significant fraud cases involving criminals stealing credit card details from banks' or companies' computer systems. Even the much-touted prospect of phoney websites, set up purely to harvest credit card details, has not proved to be a large-scale problem. Most frauds carried out online involve ordinary criminals using stolen credit card details to pay for goods and services, just as they would when buying by mail order or over the phone. In the vast majority of cases, criminals find these details on discarded paper credit card slips or by copying them from a legitimate card, rather than through the internet itself. This fact underscores the message put out by the banks and credit card companies that protection against internet fraud is largely a matter of common sense. Anyone who takes care of their credit card details is far less likely to encounter fraud, online or off.

Even so, when it comes to internet purchases and transactions, it does pay to err on the safe side simply because this relatively new marketplace can have something of the commercial Wild West about it (cowboys included). Try to keep to websites run by companies you know or recognise, and avoid sites without an address or contact phone number. For UK companies, membership of a scheme such as *Which?* Web Trader, backed by the Consumers' Association, is an added safeguard.

Legitimate e-commerce sites will use strong encryption technologies to protect credit card details in transit, and on their own systems.

Internet users should only part with their credit card details on secure sites: look for the key or padlock symbol at the bottom of the screen, and for web addresses starting https:// not just http. Never give out credit card details purely as a means of identification, and beware of putting card details in an e-mail. Hotels often ask for card details this way, but a fax or phone call is safer.

Taking simple precautions will greatly cut the risk of online card fraud, but the credit card companies recognise that consumers still lack confidence when it comes to buying online. For that reason, several cards now come with added, internet-specific features. These include guaranteed refunds in the event of *any* internet fraud losses, and added security features which promise to make card fraud that much harder.

Cahoot, for example, has launched its Webcard, which creates a new, unique number for each transaction. This means cardholders never have to give out their sensitive account details over the internet.

Extra fraud and security guarantees are not the sole preserve of the online banks, however. Companies such as Barclaycard also offer full protection against fraudulent internet transactions, as well as the ability to manage the credit card account itself online.

Online credit cards

There are now a number of credit cards that you apply for online, set up payments for online, and can only access a statement online – you no longer get the monthly paper statement. The advantage of the online statement is that you can monitor your spending at any time, rather than having to wait for the normal monthly statement.

In addition, online credit cards – available from the likes of Smile, Cahoot and Egg – have tended to offer lower rates than their offline counterparts. Online cards are able to cut interest rates by cutting administration costs. Part of this is by doing away with paper statements; part is by only allowing payment by direct debit or via online banking. When everything goes well, most people welcome cutting down on paperwork. However, cardholders have sometimes found that they could not access their statements online, and so were unable to pay off their balances on time. In other cases contacting customer services on matters such as a change of address or a higher credit limit has been less easy than it should have been.

The banks, though, have taken steps to address these problems. As internet technologies have matured, problems such as congested websites have reduced, making online cards an attractive option, especially for people able to actively manage their money.

Barclaycard (www.barclaycard.co.uk)

Barclaycard was the first credit card in the UK and still has the most customers. Barclaycard interest rates are at the higher end of the spectrum, but for cardholders who pay off their balances each month the extra services and guarantees make it a popular choice. Barclaycard offers a guarantee against online fraud – customers will have all their money refunded as long as they have not been negligent – as well as Reward points, a discounted internet access service, and online shopping price comparisons. The card's website itself provides basic account management features.

Cahoot (www.cahoot.com)

Cahoot's web card uses a unique code for each transaction, so customers never have to give out their account details over the internet. This makes the card perhaps the most secure way to shop online. Security technology aside, though, the Cahoot (plastic) credit card is typical of the current generation of internet cards: a very competitive interest rate, but no paper statements or payments through bank branches.

Egg (www.egg.com)

Egg was one of the pioneers of the internet-only credit card and has persuaded a substantial number of people to switch, not least through its 0 per cent introductory interest rate offers. Egg gives cashback on purchases as well as an internet shopping guarantee, making it attractive for people who pay off their balances too. But these services are not as unusual as they were when Egg launched.

IF (www.if.com)
Halifax-run IF has opted for a card with a generally competitive interest rate, rather than special introductory offers. One of its best features, for cardholders who are not good about managing their money, is its balance offset feature. IF can set savings or current account balances against the card balance, dramatically cutting cardholders' interest bills if they have savings as well.

RBS (www.rbs.co.uk)
Of the mainstream banks, RBS could well have the largest range of credit card deals, with a wide range of features and interest rates. RBS' card rates regularly undercut offers sent through direct mail or even the online-only cards, but cardholders can also deal with the company on the phone in the conventional way. The website has a good set of savings calculators.

Smile (www.smile.co.uk)
Smile has followed the electronic payment/online statement route with its credit card. The bank's best rate is reserved for customers who also have a Smile current account. Banking customers can pay their bills through online banking or by a direct debit for the whole balance. But with no cashback, points or other benefits, it is not a great deal for cardholders who pay their bills in full each month.

Loans

Because they are such simple financial products, personal loans are a natural for the web. Many lenders now allow applications via the internet, while online calculators allow borrowers to work out the cost of different repayment scenarios.

become financially connected with Sainsbury's bank

These days, everyone's going online to take control of their finances.
And one of the best places to start is at www.sainsburysbank.co.uk

THERE'S A BIG, WIDE WORLD ON THE WORLD-WIDE WEB. And with so much information at your fingertips it can be difficult to find the most useful sites.

However, if you're looking for financial information, you'll welcome the addition of www.sainsburysbank.co.uk.

Make Sainsbury's Bank website your first port of call and you'll be in for a surprise. Have you've ever wondered how much a loan for your dream car would cost - then realised it's 10pm and your bank is shut? If so, you'll appreciate the convenience of simply logging on and working out your budget within minutes. You could even apply online and get a decision within minutes.

An award winning Sainsbury's Bank loan could be the ideal way to afford the things you've been dreaming of! Whether it's a new car, an exotic holiday or those home improvements you've been thinking of getting on with.

You can borrow any amount between £1,000 and £15,000, helping you put the things you want within reach now.

The beauty of the internet is being able to find out what you want when you want. With a homepage which provides access to a range of financial products, you will find this website easy to use and full of helpful information. Sainsbury's Bank were awarded 'Best Internet Loans Provider 2001' by Your Money magazine so you can be sure that financial services from a trusted brand have never been so rewarding.

Take the Sainsbury's Bank Visa card, for instance. In fact, take it wherever you go – it's accepted at over 17 million outlets around the world. With a special introductory APR for six months (making it ideal for balance transfers) and competitive standard rates, it's one of the most convenient and flexible ways to pay for things when you need a little help.

A Sainsbury's Bank Visa card means you get free cover for loss or damage for almost all your purchases. And, as it's a Sainsbury's Bank Visa card, you'll earn Reward Points every time you use it.

To see the entire range of Sainsbury's Bank products make sure you visit www.sainsburysbank.co.uk the next time you're online. And discover a bank rich in good ideas.

Credit and Visa account are provided, subject to status, by Sainsbury's Bank plc. City House, City Road, Chester CH88 3AN. Written quotations are available on request. To apply, you must be at least 18 and a UK resident (excluding the Channel Islands and the Isle of Man). Sainsbury's Bank subscribes to the Banking Code: copies available on request.

Sainsbury's Bank is a registered trademark of Sainsbury's Bank plc. Teviot House, 41 South Gyle Crescent, Edinburgh EH12 9BD. Sainsbury's Bank plc, Registered Office, 33 Holborn, London EC1N 2HT. A company incorporated in England. Registered No. 3279730

Information is available in large print, audio or Braille on request, please ask for details.

You can contact us using Type Talk.

Loans

Make it happen - call Loanmakers

HOMEOWNERS ONLY

0800 027 7711

- Any purpose loans from **£3,000** to **£100,000**
- Fast, friendly, efficient service
- Consolidation loans
- All enquiries on a no obligation basis
- For an up to date quote, phone us or visit our website at **www.loanmakers.co.uk**

LOANMAKERS

Helping to make a brighter future

Your home is at risk if you do not keep up repayments on a mortgage or other loans secured on it.
Written quotations on request

5-7 Chryston House
Cloverhill Place
Chryston G69 9DQ

Websites like FT Your Money (www.ftyourmoney.com) and Moneysupermarket (www.moneysupermarket.com) will help you find the best-value loan which, when insurance and other differences are taken into account, is not necessarily the same as the lowest quoted interest rate.

Creditworthiness

Loan companies do, however, report high rejection rates for online applications, suggesting that for many people the internet is just another desperate avenue to get credit. Borrowers should be aware that applying for credit from a lot of sources can damage their credit status, while being rejected for credit may well further damage their creditworthiness.

To check your creditworthiness, try one or other of the two main credit reference agencies – **Experian** (www.uk.experian.com) and **Equifax** (www.equifax.co.uk) – which lenders consult when making loan decisions. Both websites explain credit references and allow you to apply online for your personal file.

Consumer Credit Counselling Service (www.cccs.co.uk) (0800 138 1111)
While this debt counselling charity deals primarily over the phone, its website does give details of its service.

Citizens Advice Bureaux, which can be located through www.nacab.org.uk, will also give advice to people with debt problems.

7

Mortgages and Property

Property is the single biggest purchase Britons make and a mortgage the biggest financial transaction. The internet can help you find a property or research an area to live in. It is estimated that at least a half of all properties for sale can now be viewed in some form on the internet.

In theory you could also save on estate agents' traditional commission rates by selling through a web-based service. In addition, the internet can help you find a cheaper mortgage – something that could save thousands of pounds in reduced repayments.

Online mortgage application capabilities are improving and in future it should be possible to complete the entire application process and switch loans online without the need for any paperwork or other complication. That should encourage more people to remortgage – and therefore keep their loan costs down. Remortgaging is one of the easiest ways to improve your personal finances.

However, online mortgages have not taken off as fast as many other areas of finance. This has been put down to the scary size of the transaction and the perceived need for face-to-face or at least phone-based advice. Given the size of mortgage transactions, people want their hands held, goes the argument. And, of course, most of the big mortgage lenders are still easily accessible on the High Street.

Completing an online mortgage application form can also be a laborious process. Lenders' requirements for paper proofs of income and identity and the need for borrowers to sign a loan agreement – something that digital signatures should supersede – have also contributed to these transactions remaining largely offline to date.

The MarketPlace at Bradford & Bingley

At Bradford & Bingley we have always aimed to help our clients meet their financial needs with friendly information and advice. Now you can be sure you are getting the best advice from across the market with The MarketPlace at Bradford & Bingley. Our service covers the whole range of your personal finances – mortgages, investments, pensions and insurance – we also provide an invaluable overview of your financial arrangements.

Your mortgage is likely to be your biggest financial commitment. Searching for the right one can be like entering a maze as there are over a hundred different lenders offering thousands of mortgage deals – the answer is not always obvious. The lowest rate isn't always the best mortgage. Fixed, discount and capped rates can make it difficult to evaluate the best deals. Redemption penalties, flexible options and other extras can further complicate comparisons. Our mortgage advisers will listen to you and understand your needs and objectives before recommending the most suitable mortgage product for you. With our buying power, we have access to exclusive mortgage products in addition to those available on the High Street.

Likewise, if you are looking to invest your savings, plan for retirement or safeguard the future for you and your family, then you need the security of truly unbiased financial advice. Whether you are looking for the right investment, pension, or want to review each of your existing financial situation, you need to find the solutions that are best for you. Of course, you must beware that the value of your investments may go down as well as up and you may get back less than you originally invested.

When it comes to protecting your home and possessions, it makes sense to research the market to get it right. And with so many insurance policies available, it can really pay to shop around rather than stay with the same policy year after year. At The MarketPlace, we do all of that for you. Our advisers select options from the tried and tested insurers on our carefully selected panel. We'll save you the legwork of comparing different policies and prices to ensure you're getting the best deal for you.

Our advisers are trained to find out about you and what your future aspirations might be. And because we're the largest independent financial adviser on the High Street, we offer a huge range of products from other providers across the market, all of which have been thoroughly researched. Then – and only then – will we offer the right product to suit you. And because they aren't incentivised to choose one product over another, you can be rest assured that their advice is truly impartial.

Talk to one of our MarketPlace advisers and you'll benefit from our years of experience. At Bradford & Bingley, we'll find what's best for you, not us.

YOUR HOME IS AT RISK IF YOU DO NOT KEEP UP REPAYMENTS ON A MORTGAGE OR OTHER LOAN SECURED ON IT

The mortgage market has been highly competitive for quite a few years, and borrowers have not been offered particularly special deals for going online in the same way that banks and building societies have offered better rates to savers. But this is an area to watch out for in the future – were online mortgages to be priced more cheaply, the benefits for internet-savvy borrowers could be considerable.

Property sites

Property finder and estate agents' websites stand to save homebuyers a lot of time and energy in the long process of looking for the right home. Many will automatically e-mail you details of new properties, including photographs. For people moving from the other end of the country and trying to get some idea of possible areas to live in – or for those looking at holiday homes – this should be particularly useful. As internet technology improves, 'virtual walk-throughs' of properties on the web should be widely available.

Of course, none of this is ever going to replace actually visiting properties and areas, but it should make searching for a new home more efficient and potentially less time-consuming. Making exactly the right choice of where to live, rather than a compromise based on less than perfect knowledge of what's available, should also be in your financial interests.

Property websites have been criticised for being inaccurate and out of date, specifically in advertising already-sold houses and flats. In one case, researchers found that only one in eight advertised properties were still for sale. Arguably, however, such practices are no worse than what traditional estate agents have been doing for years.

Dozens of property websites sprang up in the internet boom a couple of years back, but many have now disappeared or appear not to be widely used by homebuyers.

The ideal situation would seem to be one property website that brought together all the properties for sale in an area, both those with agents and those being sold privately. Unfortunately the market appears to have developed in a fairly fragmented way, and buyers (and sellers) should probably consult a range of sites to get the best picture. Even then, the internet appears to have some way to go before it replaces visits to local agents as the best way of researching the market. Sadly there is little evidence that agents' offices are closing down or that commissions are tumbling. Moreover, while the web offers a useful research resource for buyers, there is much less evidence of swathes of sellers successfully selling properties at reduced or minimal cost over the internet.

Asserta Home (www.asserta.co.uk) (0870 241 2960)
'The UK's leading property database'. Owned by Britain's biggest insurer, CGNU.
Features include:

- search for properties for sale in your chosen area/postcode;
- find local agents to sell your property or to buy through;
- find a letting agent;
- mortgage, insurance, and utility comparison tools;
- free environmental report (flooding, subsidence etc) for chosen postcode;
- advice and help for building your own home;
- fixed-fee conveyancing quotes from a panel of six firms;
- find a local surveyor;
- find a builder;
- moving and home improvement advice.

Asserta Home also owns **www.propertyfinder.co.uk** – another property search database.

Right Move (www.rightmove.co.uk)
Claims more than one million visitors a week. Another property database for buyers, sellers and renters. Jointly owned by a number of estate agency chains.
Features include:

- sellers can find an agent, buyers and tenants can look for properties;
- sends e-mails to agents of properties you are interested in;
- guides and tips for buyers, sellers, landlords and tenants.

Fish4Homes (www.fish4.co.uk) (020 8600 7000)
Developed by regional newspaper groups, Fish4Homes claims to have details of around 250,000 properties for sale. Sister services cover used cars and jobs.
Features include:

- buyers and prospective tenants can look for properties, sellers can find an agent;
- ask an expert: question and answer service.

Other property search websites include:

UK Property Gold (www.ukpg.co.uk) (01242 538300)

Homepages (www.homepages.co.uk) which offers private sales for £50+VAT. Homepages Ltd, Redholme House, Martinsend Lane, Great Missenden, Bucks HP16 9BH. Tel: 01494 865 563.

www.08004homes.com gives listings of local agents by postcode or area.

www.propertybroker.com, which covers London and the South East, will advertise your property for £97, including putting up a For Sale board. You do the showing and selling, and pay no agents' commission.

www.loot.com is the website of the well-known small ads newspaper. It also has a private sales service.

Choosing an area

Here the internet's research capabilities should come into their own. As well as these websites, you could look at the websites of local newspapers, councils and tourist offices.

Up My Street (www.upmystreet.co.uk)
Highly-acclaimed local information and services website. Details of pubs, restaurants, transport links, education and crime figures, council performance, even a profile of the typical resident, all by postcode. Includes maps.

www.wheretomove.co.uk
This site will e-mail area guides, including transport details, council tax bands etc.

Property market information

House price indexes are widely followed, but inevitably the press summaries can be misleading because of their big-picture take on the market. Much of the information that makes up the headline numbers is available on the internet, allowing homebuyers to find the more meaningful 'nitty gritty' figures for particular types of properties in specific localities – ie what they are actually trying to buy.

Land Registry (www.landreg.gov.uk)
The government department responsible for registering property ownership. As well as giving and keeping details of who owns what, it also publishes authoritative quarterly property price data.

Hometrack (www.hometrack.co.uk) (0800 019 4440)
Gives details of price movements by postcode and property type. Other analysis of local property markets includes changes in the number of properties for sale (measured by estate agent instructions); number of

buyers registered; time to sell and number of viewings taken to make a sale. Information for its 'Hometrack Index' is provided by estate agents. Updated monthly. Aimed at homeowners and homebuyers.

Halifax House Price Index figures are at www.hbosplc.com and as well as monthly and quarterly price movements there is an online house price calculator for average price changes over a chosen period.

Rival **Nationwide Building Society** also produces widely followed statistics on property price movements. Monthly and quarterly reports are at www.nationwide.co.uk (see also Mortgage Lenders section for websites of these two home loan giants).

Buy-to-let

Association of Residential Letting Agents (Arla) (www.arla.co.uk) (0845 345 5752) Arla, Maple House, 53–55 Woodside Road, Amersham, Bucks HP6 6AA.
Promoters of buy-to-let property investment, an increasingly popular alternative to traditional pension plans.
Features include:

- advice and information on buy-to-let, including mortgages;
- find a local letting agent;
- advice and information for landlords;
- advice and information for tenants.

Buy-to-Let-UK (www.buy-to-let-uk.co.uk)
Tips, advice and local rental market information.

See also **www.inlandrevenue.gov.uk** for information on the taxation of rent – search on its website for leaflets IR87 and IR150.

Want to take a leap into the
property market?

If you're thinking about hopping onto the investment property ladder, then Skipton's Buy-To-Let Mortgage could be just what you're looking for.

With mortgage interest rates being so low and stock market investments generally performing badly, there has never been a better time to buy property to let out privately.

For more information on our latest Buy-To-Let Mortgages visit our website at www.skipton.co.uk or call 08457 171777

SKIPTON
BUILDING SOCIETY

www.skipton.co.uk

YOUR HOME IS AT RISK IF YOU DO NOT KEEP UP REPAYMENTS ON A MORTGAGE OR OTHER LOAN SECURED ON IT.

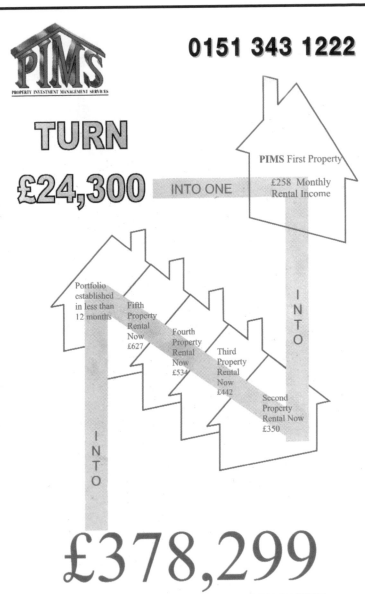

Property Search Agency (www.thepropertyforum.net)
PSA does environmental and local authority searches but probably more interesting for its website's property market/industry news.

Mortgage lenders

The Council of Mortgage Lenders (www.cml.org.uk)
This has a range of useful publications and factsheets on homebuying and mortgages.

Halifax (www.halifax.co.uk) (08456 00 10 00)
Britain's biggest lender, its website features:

- step-by-step guide through the homebuying process, including tools to calculate how much you can borrow, what your repayments will be, and how much you can afford to pay each month. Includes the ability to get an online 'Mortgage Promise' – a conditional offer – in minutes, a homebuyers' checklist (for printing off and taking on viewings), and a Mortgage Enquirer to keep track online of how your loan application is progressing;
- details of available Halifax mortgages;
- apply for home insurance online and get a discount;
- Halifax HomeFinder shows properties for sale in 350+ Halifax branches.

Nationwide Building Society (www.nationwide.co.uk) (08457 30 20 10)
Britain's biggest mutual mortgage lender, which means the society is owned by its customers (called members) who, depending on your point of view, stand to receive a windfall at some stage in the future or who should get a better deal by dint of being part-owners of the business (or maybe both!).
Features include:

Over 800 listings for
our 'best buy' mortgages
in 2001

Why not visit
www.thenottingham.com

NOTTINGHAM
BUILDING SOCIETY

Nottingham House, 5/13 Upper Parliament Street, Nottingham NG1 2BX
Telephone: 0115 948 1444   Fax: 0115 948 3948
www.thenottingham.com
e-mail: sales-development@thenottingham.com

I'd like to find a way to cut 6 years off our mortgage.

I'd like to know it's not going to cost us anything extra.

People
With
ideas

OFFSET MORTGAGES . SAVINGS POTS . OVERNIGHT SWEEPING . MULTI-CHANNEL ACCESS

open plan
from THE WOOLWICH

0845 607 1111
www.thewoolwich.co.uk

You're either with us. Or without.

Halifax Online offers you an easy and secure way to manage your money over the Internet, day or night

Here are just some of the things you can do on Halifax Online:

HALIFAX BANK ACCOUNT	Apply for an account, view transactions, pay bills, transfer funds and more
WEB SAVER	An easy way to manage your savings
SHARE DEALING	Deal in real time online with low dealing charges and free market information
CREDIT CARDS	View transactions and current credit limit, change payment details and more
HOLIDAY MONEY	Order currency and traveller's cheques online, providing you have a suitable Halifax account
SAVINGS ACCOUNTS	View statements, make funds transfers, view interest rates
FINANCIAL PORTFOLIO	See most of your Halifax accounts together on one screen when you create your own financial portfolio

Once you have registered for Halifax Online and set up your accounts you can take advantage of our **financial portfolio** feature which helps you to organise your finances quickly and simply.

This tool allows you to see information about most of your Halifax accounts together on one screen. You can add or remove accounts from view on your portfolio whenever you like and can even set it as your default screen.

Security and privacy

As you would expect, when it comes to looking after your money, we do everything we can to ensure it's safe. Not only that, we make sure we act responsibly in terms of looking after the information we hold about you and that you're kept fully informed of anything that may affect you.

When it comes to our online application forms and Halifax Online – our Internet banking service – we make use of the highest security measures available to us. And to ensure you have no concerns about the safety of your money, we make the following guarantee:

'If a Halifax Online customer is a victim of fraud we guarantee that they won't lose any money on their Halifax account and will always be reimbursed in full.'

And that's not all:

- Halifax Online and our online application forms use 128-bit encryption, the highest level of security available. This ensures information is virtually impossible for anyone else to read unless they have the 'key' or password.
- There's a secure communications link, called a Secure Socket Layer (SSL), which encrypts all the information passed between your browser and Halifax Online.
- Free anti-virus software, normally selling at £20, is available to all registered Halifax Online users. Regular updates are also provided.

fulfil your dreams...

...the Lambeth's taking care of it
MORTGAGES

08000 28 69 28

■Lambeth
BUILDING SOCIETY

www.lambeth.co.uk

Time is of the essence – and so is your money

We know that time is a precious commodity and that applying for a mortgage or managing your account is not always feasible during "normal" business hours – after all, most of us are working ourselves at this time!

That's why at Britannic Money we offer a host of online facilities enabling you to logon and research our mortgages, apply online and receive an Agreement-In-Principle in just 20 minutes.

Once your mortgage has completed you can manage your account online at a time and pace that suits you. You can check your account balance, order statements, use our online mortgage calculator to see how much you can save by adjusting your mortgage payments, arrange for bills to be paid and order cheque books. You can also see a breakdown of your income and expenditure with our balance sheet and cash-flow.

It all starts at our website www.britannicmoney.com

Just as you like to use your time efficiently, with a Britannic Money flexible mortgage you can make your money work more efficiently too.

Why not logon and take a look at our multiple award winning mortgages. For the fifth year in a row, Britannic Money has won the coveted 'Best Flexible Mortgage' award at this year's Your Mortgage Awards, and also scooped the new category 'Best CAM/Offset Mortgage' to add to our collection.

Find out how you can get your money working harder today. Logon to our website at www.britannicmoney.com or call us on 0800 550 551. Lines are open 8am – 8pm weekdays, 9am – 5pm Saturdays.

Voted the Best Flexible Mortgage 5 years running!

YOUR MORTGAGE
www.yourmortgage.co.uk

2001~2002 AWARDS

**BEST
FLEXIBLE
MORTGAGE**

BRITANNIC MONEY

Listen to the experts.

Every year 100 mortgage intermediaries vote in the Your Mortgage Magazine Awards. And every year for the past 5 years they've recognised our flexible mortgages as the best for borrowers.

To see what Britannic Money can do for you call us now.

0800 550 551 or visit
www.britannicmoney.com

britannic money

- details of available mortgages, online applications (and how to apply more traditionally), and a facility to view the balance and payments for your existing Nationwide mortgage online. Guides to buying a home, applying for credit, and a jargon buster. Also tools for calculating how much you can borrow, how much the mortgage you want will cost, and a calculator for working out how much your home could be worth;
- quotes and sales of home and buildings insurance;
- Gateway to the Web feature has other Home & Garden information.

For other lenders search under name using a search engine such as www.google.co.uk or a financial directory such as Find (www.find.co.uk). There is a listing of building societies in Chapter 3.

Mortgage brokers and comparison information

With more than 100 lenders offering 4,000-plus mortgage variations, choosing the best value home loan – which does not just mean the lowest interest rate – is a Herculean task. In the past, most people haven't even bothered to try – they have simply compared mortgages from a couple of the big High Street lenders. Mortgage brokers have long offered advice and recommendations – but at a fee of up to 1 per cent of the loan value. The great boon of the internet is that borrowers have free access to comparison tools and information that allows them to choose the best-value mortgage for themselves.

Charcol (www.charcolonline.co.uk) (0800 71 81 91)
Britain's biggest mortgage broker, owned by Bradford & Bingley. Features 500 mortgages from 50 lenders.
The website includes:

- best-buys for first-time buyers, remortgages and buy-to-let loans;
- mortgage 'wizard' to help find the right deal for you;

- online applications;
- waives its normal commission on mortgages (up to 1 per cent of loan value) applied for through website;
- Call Me function for immediate phone help;
- tools: how much X mortgage at Y rate will cost per month; how much you can borrow; overpayment calculator for showing how much quicker a mortgage could be paid off;
- includes exclusive Charcol-only mortgage deals from leading lenders;
- useful 'learn about' guides, including the homebuying process, remortgaging, buy-to-let;
- insurance services.

Charcol also runs the mortgage finder services of a number of other websites. These can be worth looking at in addition to Charcol's own site. For example, www.tesco.com, the website of Britain's biggest supermarket, offers a number of exclusive 'Tesco Specials'.

Other mortgage broker sites include:

London & Country (www.lcplc.co.uk) which has tools for assessing whether a remortgage is worthwhile. London & Country Mortgages, Beazer House, Lower Bristol Road, Bath BA2 3BA; 0800 373300.

Creditweb (www.creditweb.co.uk) which offers a £150 cashback through its Employee Partnership Programme to borrowers who work for certain companies. Creditweb, Elizabeth House, 39 York Road, London SE1 7NQ; 0800 358 3388.

Moneysupermarket (www.moneysupermarket.com) which has a Mortgage Auction feature where lenders bid better terms on £150,000+ mortgages. Money Supermarket, 1 Chantry Court, Sovereign Way, Chester, Cheshire CH1 4QA; 0845 345 5708.

Moneyfacts (www.moneyfacts.co.uk) – the 'rate bible' of the finance industry which provides most of the best-buy tables for national newspapers. As well as best-buys, the service has a search facility. Also has a Property section in its Information Channel.

Mortgage insurance

Most mortgage lenders will try to sell you various types of mortgage and home insurance. The main mortgage insurance is commonly called mortgage protection or mortgage payment protection and covers your monthly repayments, but others include Mig (Mortgage Indemnity Guarantee) insurance, which, in fact, protects the lender rather than the borrower – even though you pay for it! Chapter 9 also gives details of insurers who will offer cover for mortgages, home contents and buildings.

Specialist websites include **www.insureyourmortgage.co.uk www.protectyourmortgage.co.uk** and **www.takeshelter.co.uk**

Homebuying/homeowning services

Improveline (www.improveline.com)
Find a reliable and recommended builder, plumber or other tradesman. 150,000 screened firms/workmen. The site asks customers to review firms they have used – reviews that can be accessed on the site. It also includes an ask the expert function and design and project management help.

I Have Moved (www.ihavemoved.com)
Free service for changing billing details with up to 750 organisations, from utilities to magazine publishers to the DVLA and other government bodies.

www.simplymove.co.uk is similar.

www.self-build.co.uk
For information and advice on building your own home.

www.solicitors-online.com
www.lawyerlocator.co.uk
For finding solicitors for conveyancing.

To find a surveyor, go to the **National Network of Chartered Surveyors and Valuers** at www.surveyline.co.uk

To find a removal company, the **British Association of Removers** is at www.bar.co.uk or go to www.yell.com

Watchdogs

Ombudsman for Estate Agents (www.oea.co.uk) (01722 333 306)
For complaining about estate agents. Gives details of the code of practice estate agents should abide by, and arbitrates in disputes.

Mortgage Code Compliance Board (www.mortgagecode.co.uk)
For information on complaining about mortgage brokers and lenders.

The National House-Building Council (www.nhbc.co.uk)
This has details of its charter regulating the construction of new homes, with a guide to making a complaint.

8

Account Aggregation

Account aggregation is both potentially one of the most interesting and most controversial areas of internet finance. It might not be a term that trips off the tongue, but account aggregation is not a complicated concept. At its simplest, it lets individuals bring all their financial information together on one computer screen or web page. The idea is to make managing money easier: it should take no more than a few mouse clicks to transfer funds between accounts, pay bills or even deal in stocks and shares.

How an aggregation service works

At its simplest, such services give users a single screen that details balances and transactions for all their bank accounts and savings. The systems can also support investments, either in individual shares or in funds such as investment trusts.

MyAccounts, the aggregation service run by Citibank in the UK, also supports information from a number of utility companies, so users can also manage their household bills via the service. It will even detail information from Frequent Fliers' programmes.

The precise features on offer from aggregators vary – and are likely to change over time. Initially, only a small number of banks and brokers supported Citibank's service. This means that although users can track their share prices online, they cannot trade with all stockbrokers from within the Citibank website. This is because account aggregation raises some important questions about both privacy and security. The Financial Services Authority (FSA), the chief financial watchdog, has warned consumers to tread very warily when it comes to using aggregators. Along with APACS, the body that regulates inter-bank money transfers, the FSA has even suggested that the way some services work means they could be breaking data protection laws.

Aggregration websites use one of two methods to gather all the data they need: direct data feeds from the banks, and 'screen scraping'. The latter is a technique where computers, owned by the aggregation website, log on to banks' websites on behalf of account holders, and then copy the information on to their own databases. They either do this at pre-set intervals, or when the user logs on to the aggregation service. Screen scraping is controversial, because it can be done without the consent of the banks. In the wrong hands, it could also pose real security problems for accountholders. Once an individual hands over their username and password for an online bank account, they are very exposed should that information fall into the wrong hands.

Moreover, by putting all their financial information into one place, they run the risk that if a hacker or criminal does break in, all their financial information for all their accounts will be open to abuse. And the rules for fraud compensation might not protect account aggregation customers because they have given information that should be secret – such as a PIN numbers – to a third party.

Account aggregation is already big business in the US, where more than two million people have signed up to one of the services on offer. Here, it has been longer in coming. Citibank launched its service in 2001 but other banks' plans have taken longer to materialise. Virgin Money, for example, has put its plans on hold for the present time, although Egg still plans to launch a service. Banking industry experts reckon that most, if not all, UK banks have systems in place to handle account aggregation, but that most have pulled back from a public launch, at least until the legal and regulatory position becomes clearer.

Developments in technology could help solve some of the problems around aggregation. The way in which banks handle their data internally is changing, with most moving to systems that work more closely with the internet. These new systems are far better placed to communicate with each other, making it much easier for account aggregators to base their services around data feeds rather than screen scraping.

For accountholders, data feeds have some important advantages. If an account aggregator sets up a data feed with a bank or share dealing service, they will be covered by industry compensation schemes should something go wrong. Banks, in turn, are unlikely to hand over customer information unless they are happy that it is secure. Feeds will be turned on or off on the basis of deals between the banks or between the banks and standalone aggregation companies. As long as the bank is happy that a customer has signed up for the aggregation service, it will turn on the supply of his or her account information to the aggregator. The aggregator will have its own security measures in place to protect the data. There is no need for the customer to give online banking passwords to the aggregator, and no need for them to be stored in the aggregation computer.

Data feeds should also be quicker and more reliable than screen scraping; one criticism banks have levied at account aggregation is that the screen scraping process could put out-of-date information onto the aggregator's websites. These developments need the co-operation of competing banks, however, and it will take time before all the rival companies agree the rules for aggregation and sign up. In the meantime, though, there is another way to bring savings, investment and current account information together in one place – by using personal finance software.

Personal finance software packages

Computer software packages such as Microsoft Money and Quicken have sophisticated features for managing portfolios and accounts, in much the same way as online account aggregation sites. The difference is that users download their account information onto their own computers, so there is no need to give out personal information to third parties.

Several banks directly support file exchange with Microsoft Money or Quicken, and others support data in Excel spreadsheet format, which can then be copied across. This is one of the safest ways to bring together financial data, as users log on to their online banking sites in the normal way, choose what to download, and then move the details into the financial package. Microsoft Money has a specific Online Services Manager function for banking.

As well as bringing together information from several accounts, packages such as Microsoft Money and Quicken have other useful features, including mortgage calculators and systems for managing dividend income, as well as support for tax return information. Depending on the version and its features, both packages start at under £50. Once the information is on the computer, users' data is as secure as the machine itself; so although it makes sense to set a password for the computer, there are few real security risks.

Account aggregation sites
Citibank: www.citibank.co.uk

Personal finance software
Microsoft Money: www.microsoft.com/uk/homepc/money
Quicken: www.intuit.co.uk/quicken/

9

Insurance

Insurance lends itself to buying online. For years, the insurance industry has sold its policies over the phone; buying on the internet is the logical next step. After all, almost everyone finds buying insurance a chore. Shopping around for policies is even more tedious: getting a motor quote on the phone could easily take half an hour per insurance company. The internet should cut out all this and give policyholders a better deal too. Unfortunately for consumers, the internet's impact on the insurance world has been less than revolutionary. A few years ago, new insurance websites seemed to launch almost weekly. More recently, the story has been one of consolidation. Standalone websites have closed, and others have merged or been taken over by banks or other insurance brokers. This, coupled with further mergers in the insurance industry itself, has led to less choice not more; insurance premiums are generally rising too.

The good news is that there is scarcely any insurance policy that cannot be bought online. Household (building and contents), motoring and travel cover are still the most widely bought policies, but there are websites offering more specialist insurance as well as life cover. The large general insurers are adding to their internet offerings too, with most selling household, motor, travel and even pet insurance via their websites. Online insurance websites are open around the clock and, assuming you have a credit or debit card you can get a quote and take out the policy immediately – useful for buying travel insurance the night before you go on holiday, for example. This 'open all hours' approach also has the great advantage that there is no 'hard sell' and no pressure to sign up there and then.

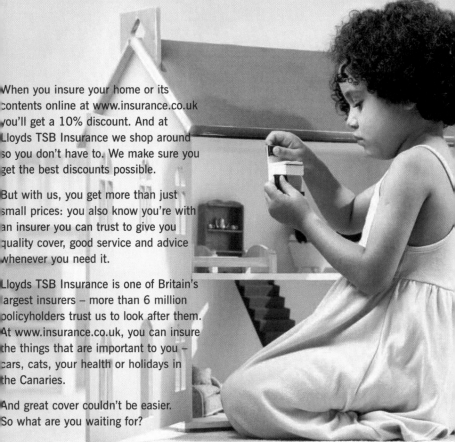

great insurance small prices

get 10% discount on your home insurance when you buy online at www.insurance.co.uk

When you insure your home or its contents online at www.insurance.co.uk you'll get a 10% discount. And at Lloyds TSB Insurance we shop around so you don't have to. We make sure you get the best discounts possible.

But with us, you get more than just small prices: you also know you're with an insurer you can trust to give you quality cover, good service and advice whenever you need it.

Lloyds TSB Insurance is one of Britain's largest insurers – more than 6 million policyholders trust us to look after them. At www.insurance.co.uk, you can insure the things that are important to you – cars, cats, your health or holidays in the Canaries.

And great cover couldn't be easier. So what are you waiting for?

www.insurance.co.uk

General Insurance advice is provided by Lloyds TSB Insurance Services Limited. Registered in England No 968406 71 Lombard Street London EC3P 3BS. Member of the General Insurance Standards Council.

 **Insurance**

AXAHOME.CO.UK
a place for everything

"It's easier to manage things when they're all in one place . . ."

axahome.co.uk is the unique website from AXA; one of the world's largest insurers, serving 40 million customers in 60 countries.

axahome is the quick and easy way to take care of your home management needs, giving you complete control from just one place.

As well as offering an extensive range of insurance products, such as Motor, Home, Pet, Home Emergency and Private Medical insurance, axahome also offers services to help you manage your life, for instance, Unsecured Personal Loans, Holidays, Flights, and Home Security Systems.

The site is designed with speed and simplicity in mind. User-friendly navigation and a dedicated customer service team make using axahome.co.uk a breeze.

A straightforward and competitive Home insurance quote is available in less than 5 minutes and our award winning online Motor insurance service can provide you with a quote in less time than it takes to boil an egg! Your quotes can be saved for future use and are easy to retrieve.

Visit www.axahome.co.uk to see how AXA can make life easier.

Legal & General Insurance

First established over 160 years ago, Legal & General has become one of the UK's most admired and best known financial services companies. With representation in France, Holland and the USA the Group is a leading financial institution in terms of both investment and underlying financial strength managing assets worth over £113bn*. We have a strong presence in the motor and household insurance market as well as life assurance, pensions, mortgages, savings, investments, banking and healthcare products.

Legal & General Insurance recognise that your home, car and personal belongings are likely to be your most valuable assets and there is always the need to protect them adequately against the unexpected.

That's why at Legal & General we aim to provide you with the very best cover that meets your needs. Unlike many providers, with Legal & General you can choose the cover to suit you, with great value buildings and contents insurance and a competitive quote for car insurance from our panel of carefully selected insurers.

We recognise the importance of providing you with peace of mind and for that reason we offer travel insurance to cover you and your possessions whilst on holiday and a car rescue service option to cover your vehicle in the event of a breakdown in the UK.

By obtaining insurance from Legal & General we will ensure you benefit not only from flexible, value for money products but also from knowing that you have the support of one of the UK's leading insurance companies.

In just a few simple steps you could be enjoying complete insurance cover from Legal & General. Visit us at www.legalandgeneral.com.

as at 30.6.01

Legal & General Insurance Limited

Registered in England: No 423930.
Registered Office: Temple Court, 11 Queen Victoria Street, London EC4N 4TP.
A member of the Association of British Insurers and the
General Insurance Standards Council.

It is possible to compare policies carefully – most websites provide good details of cover – and see which extras and options affect the final price. These online calculator tools are useful: a cheap motor insurance policy can become quite expensive if drivers have to pay extra for legal or overseas cover or face a high excess.

To buy home insurance online, you will need some basic information to hand, such as details of your house, the sum you want to insure (for buildings and for contents) and when it was built; for motoring, you will need details of the car, its approximate value, and details of who will be driving. None of this is unique to online insurance – a broker or call centre operator will ask the same questions – but it does help to have all the documentation to hand.

On the phone or face-to-face, a trained operator or insurance broker will know exactly what information is needed, and whether any of it is less important or can be approximate. But on the internet, buyers are on their own. Some websites have done little to present forms designed for professionals in a user-friendly way. Even the best-designed insurance websites can be confusing in places.

The information insurance companies need and the way their forms are designed is at its trickiest for motor insurance. Some sites have huge 'drop-down' menus of car makes and models, for example, but little or nothing to help the driver whose exact car is not listed. Some home insurance sites still ask for the exact year a house was built: unless you live in a new home this is information you might well not have. This sort of information might seem trivial, but entering the wrong details into an online form will affect premiums – sometimes significantly. Worse still, it could render a policy invalid when it comes to making a claim.

The big-name insurers have done the best jobs of making their websites easy to use, and most have helpdesks that can answer queries from users without forcing them to go through all the information again with a telesales operator.

At the other end of the spectrum, some of the smaller companies' and brokers' sites are notorious for cryptic error messages and requests to call helpdesks that are permanently busy or never return calls. Others produce inviting initial 'quotes' based on simple information, only to quote a much higher price or refuse cover altogether once buyers have filled in the whole form. Perhaps fortunately, some of the worst sites have gone out of business in the last year to 18 months. Others have cleaned up their acts.

However, if you have an unusual car, a risky occupation, or a house with a thatched roof, the internet might not be the best place to look for insurance. In those cases a conventional broker is probably still the best option. And if the prospect of endless form filling sounds uninviting, there is still a good reason to look for insurance online – put simply, that is cost. Insurers offer discounts to policyholders who sign up online, and the few remaining online brokers also promise good deals. The savings can be significant, including for drivers or homeowners who are already with a 'big name' insurer and who do not want to switch. Norwich Union offers up to 10 per cent internet discount on its policies; Royal & SunAlliance, through its More Th>n brand, offers a 2.5 per cent discount for new home policies booked online. Organising all your insurance over the internet could save more than £100.

The savings should be greater still from a smaller 'direct' insurer or through an online broker. Companies such as Direct Line promise to beat rival household cover prices by as much as 25 per cent, although they also claim significant savings for customers who buy on the phone. Online insurance brokers should be able to produce even better deals, because they can scan the whole market for the best policy. However, the number of independent insurance websites has fallen quite sharply since the height of the internet boom. Of those that remain, many select their policies from a quite limited panel of insurers. Sometimes, policies can even be more expensive, showing how important it is to shop around. Exceptions include some of the more specialist companies: for the over-50s, for example, SAGA often appears to come up with reasonable insurance deals.

Price, however, is not the only criteria for buying insurance. Standards of service, especially claims handling, also matter. There is no way to tell this from a website, but internet users should still check that their rights are safeguarded. The most important check to make is that the insurer is a member of the General Insurance Standards Council; its logo will be on member websites. Both insurance companies and brokers can be members. If a website is for an insurance broker, the company might also be a member of the British Insurance Brokers Association (BIBA), which also has a code of practice. Finally, only part with credit or debit card details via a secure website.

Insurance brokers

The AA (www.theaa.co.uk)
Although best known as a motoring organisation, the AA is also a significant insurance broker. The company sells motor, home and travel insurance policies as well as bike and commercial vehicle cover. The site carries an index of insurance premiums, which is a useful way to check whether your rates are still competitive.

Direct Choice (www.directchoice.co.uk)
Broker Direct Choice has a good reputation in the insurance industry for competitive premiums. The company offers travel, household and motor cover, including bikes, as well as van insurance and cover for tradesmen. Direct Choice selects policies from 20 insurers, which helps keep rates keen.

Insure.co.uk (www.insure.co.uk)
Insure.co.uk is web-only, although it is backed by a conventional insurance broker, Boncaster. Like many of the broker-backed sites, Insure.co.uk selects policies from a panel of household name insurers. The website uses six companies and provides motor, household, travel and car breakdown cover.

InsuranceWide (www.insurancewide.co.uk)
InsuranceWide started out as a standard online insurance broker, but now provides policies from other brokers, general insurance companies

and insurers that usually only sell direct. The idea is that users' queries are passed on to the best insurer or broker, based on simple online forms. This is a particularly good website for specialist policies. InsuranceWide will cover a wide range of businesses, high-value homes and it has specific insurance for computers, including an excess-free policy for laptops.

Screentrade (www.screentrade.co.uk)
Screentrade was one of the first internet-only insurance brokers, and is now owned by Lloyds TSB. It offers home, car and travel cover and the service is quick.

Home and motor insurance

Admiral (www.admiral-insurance.co.uk)
Admiral specialises in lower-cost car insurance for people living in and around London. The website has other more unusual features too. These include physiotherapy cover and complementary therapy cover. Admiral offers travel, car breakdown and household insurance, all with online quotes.

Churchill (www.churchill.co.uk)
Churchill sells its travel, pet insurance, motor and household policies over the internet, and offers a 5 per cent discount for buying online. The website has online claim tracking; unusually visitors can also watch Churchill's TV ads (with the talking bulldog) and buy Churchill souvenirs.

Cornhill Direct (www.cornhilldirect.co.uk)
Cornhill provides car and van cover, household insurance and life cover through its website. The company offers discounts to the over-50s; the main site (www.cornhill.co.uk) has details of wedding and musical instrument cover, mostly sold through brokers.

Buy home insurance sitting at your desk

And we'll cover your behind

Hiscox Online is the leading online specialist UK home insurance service. It has been designed to suit those of you who lead busy lives, and want efficiency, reliability, service and good value from your insurer. Hiscox Online is available for people with higher value homes (contents worth over £50,000). You could be pleasantly surprised at how little insurance providing superior cover costs and how quickly and easily it can be arranged.

What's the catch?
You would have thought that all the extra cover would come at a price, but specialist insurance can actually work out cheaper than a standard insurance policy.
We are selective about who we insure and our customers tend to look after their possessions better, resulting in fewer claims and lower premiums.

Save time, online
Hiscox Online is the only site in the UK where you can buy, manage and update your policy securely, totally online. A Quick Quote can be obtained in 30 seconds and if you want to continue, a full application will be processed in less than 5 minutes. No tedious piles of paper - everything can be completed online.

Is specialist insurance for me?
Specialist household insurance is specifically designed to meet the needs of those who value their possessions. Run-of-the-mill insurance policies usually only cover you for a maximum of £1,000 for a single item. Specialist insurance offers higher, or no, insurance limits for each individual item and will cover you for all risks.

Features and Benefits
- Comprehensive cover: we offer worldwide cover inside and outside the home as standard (includes accidental damage and accidental loss)

- Excellent claims service

- Quick and easy: get a quote, buy and manage online

- Service oriented: 24 hour query turnaround

- Access to expert advice

- Underwritten by Hiscox, the UK's leading specialist insurer

For more information and to get a Quick Quote, simply go to:

www.hiscox.com/mm

HISCOX

Direct Line (www.directline.co.uk)
Famously, Direct Line was one of the first companies to sell insurance only by phone in the UK, undercutting policies sold through brokers. Direct Line has recently redesigned its website, and it now has one of the simplest application forms, especially for car insurance.

Eagle Star (www.eaglestar.co.uk)
Visitors to Eagle Star's website are greeted by a virtual assistant, Catherine. The policies on offer follow the usual travel, motor and household route, but the company also includes boat cover. Policies are fully specified with plenty of extras.

Norwich Union (www.norwichunion.co.uk)
Norwich Union encourages policyholders to book online by giving a 10 per cent discount off travel, household and car insurance premiums. The company also sells life assurance, critical illness and accidental death cover through the site, as well as motorcycle insurance and domestic appliance breakdown. Overall, the site is clear and easy to use.

Prudential (www.pru.co.uk)
The Pru made its name selling insurance door-to-door. Today, the internet insurance operation looks a little thin compared with the competition, with just home and motor cover on offer. But the company's site is easy to use, and the Pru's home insurance policy offers £6,000 of home office cover as standard.

Royal & SunAlliance (More Th>n) (www.morethan.com)
Royal & SunAlliance now sells insurance through the internet under the More Th>n label. Policies on offer include home, motoring, travel, pet cover, life assurance and health cover. Quick quotes are available online; if you get stuck, More Th>n will phone you back if you click a button on the website.

Saga (www.saga.co.uk)
Saga specialises in services to the over-50s, and offers home, travel, pet and motor insurance online. The site is clear and easy to use and Saga is especially strong on some of the more unusual policies, including motorhome and caravan insurance, boat and holiday home cover.

Travel insurers

American Express (www.americanexpress.co.uk)
American Express is not the cheapest travel insurer on the market, although it is cheaper than annual policies sold by travel operators and agents. The company sells single trip policies, but most people come for the annual cover, which gives both business and personal insurance as standard. The policy also includes pre-booked trips of three days or more in the UK. The website is clear and professional.

Columbus Direct (www.columbus-direct.co.uk)
Columbus started selling travel insurance in 1988, when most people bought their cover through travel agents. The company covers up to 60 days consecutive travel, with worldwide cover for a couple starting at under £100. The website is quick and easy to use. Columbus also has a more comprehensive policy, Lifestyle, for frequent travellers as well as pet cover and car rescue.

Specialist insurers

Endsleigh (www.endsleigh.co.uk)
Endsleigh has long specialised in insurance for students, and it also has specific policies for young people who are not in education – the company says it sells insurance for 'career people'. It is one of the best places to look for cover for shared houses or halls of residence.

Elephant (www.elephant.co.uk)

Elephant specialises in motor cover, and especially in providing competitive rates for younger drivers. The website's quote forms are fairly detailed but easy to follow, and its rates are generally low. The system automatically recalculates premiums based on a higher or lower voluntary excess, or for a protected no-claims bonus. Visitors should make sure they scroll down to the bottom of the final screen, though: otherwise they will automatically opt in for junk mail.

NFU Mutual (www.nfumutual.co.uk)

NFU Mutual is closely tied to the farming world, but its policies are not restricted to farmers. In fact, the organisation offers a wide range of useful insurance options, especially for people in rural areas. Cover includes specialist policies for thatched buildings, for people working from home and horse and rider insurance. Most quotes are available online, and if you need cover for a vintage tractor, this is the place.

Bennetts Bike Insurance (www.bennetts.co.uk)

Bikers sometimes struggle to find competitive insurance, and not all of the big insurers or brokers cover two-wheeled transport. Bennetts is a specialist insurance broker that has covered motorbikes since the 1930s, and now offers full quotes over the internet.

Life and health insurance

Direct Life and Pension Services (www.directlife.co.uk)

Direct Life and Pension Services is majority-owned by the Skipton Building Society but sources policies from a wide range of life assurance companies. The website is clear, offering buttons for just two types of quote: life and critical illness cover, and accident, sickness and unemployment insurance. Quotes take just a few minutes, and the website gives clear explanations of the different insurances.

Save money. Cut the cost of your life insurance – instantly!

If you have taken out a life insurance policy recently, or are considering one now, LifeSearch could save you money. We compare hundreds of quotes from leading companies and can almost certainly get you the same cover for considerably less.

£100,000 of Life Cover

Alliance & Leicester	£22.90
M & S	£15.25
Eagle Star Direct	£14.66
Abbey National Life	£14.42
Virgin	£12.00
LifeSearch	**£9.81**

Call LifeSearch direct on

0800 316 3166

Anytime 8.00am to 8.00pm weekdays and weekends

Please quote reference MMO

www.lifesearch.co.uk

*Life***SEARCH**

We search. You save.

Premiums based on a monthly cost, with a leading insurer, for 25 year level term life cover for a non-smoking man aged 35 next birthday in normal health. Figures correct at February 2002.

Lifesearch (www.lifesearch.co.uk)

Lifesearch provides life assurance and critical illness cover either through its website or on the phone. As a discount broker, buying policies here will be cheaper than going direct to an insurer or through a financial adviser, but the company still uses big name insurance companies to provide its policies. The site has a handy premium calculator, but the company does recommend that users call to work out exactly which policy they need.

See also Chapter 10 for pension/life insurance companies and for endowment brokers.

10
Pensions

Perhaps no one will ever make pensions sexy, but the internet could do a lot to make this most-confusing of personal finance subjects more comprehensible and accessible. Unreadable pension projections sent out every year could be put online, preferably combining all your entitlements – state, workplace and personal – to give an overall picture.

The internet already has the calculator tools to illustrate how an individual's pension saving is progressing – and to show what could happen under different investment and retirement scenarios. But it is difficult to point to one website or service that brings this all together for an individual in a user-friendly way. There is also no obvious technical barrier to internet applications and access to pension entitlements with previous employers.

However, the current reality is that the online pensions industry has not developed to anything like the degree of banking, investing or even mortgages. If online mortgages have been held back by the size of the financial transaction, pensions are said to be too complicated. Individuals need personalised and face-to-face advice and therefore the internet has not been seen as the best medium – maybe. Thankfully pensions are becoming somewhat simpler with the introduction of the government-designed stakeholder plan. It is also dawning on increasing numbers of people that however complicated the subject of pensions may be, they really must get to grips with it. Increasing life expectancy, declining state help as well as cutbacks and changing employer provision all mean that individuals are having to consider how they will manage in retirement.

YOU CAN

START A

FRIENDS
PROVIDENT

STAKEHOLDER PENSION

STANDING ON
YOUR HEAD

www.friendsprovident.com

FRIENDS PROVIDENT

FRIENDS tell it like it is – *Stakeholder Pensions*

In April 2001 the government introduced "Stakeholder Pensions". But what exactly are they and what are the benefits of holding one?

Well, let's start with a few facts and figures:

- In the UK more than 40% of social security spending goes on state pensions. (Note 1)
- There is no underlying fund supporting these payments – pensions for today's pensioners, are paid for by today's working population.
- Our life expectancy is ever improving – that means that the number of pensioners is increasing and therefore so is the cost.

The serious question is – will tomorrow's workers be able to support you in your retirement?

What is a stakeholder pension?
To face these challenges the Government introduced stakeholder pension schemes. These are intended to encourage individuals to increase their private retirement savings by offering them a simple, cheap and flexible pension plan.

But there are two important things which have changed with the introduction of stakeholder pensions:

Firstly, the tax benefits that were given to working people are now available to everyone, working or not, under 75 years of age.
And secondly, companies like ours that manage people's pensions are being forced to keep our charges low – under 1% of the value of the fund - which means in many cases people are going to get better value for money.

Why should I buy a stakeholder pension?
There are a number of reasons why you should consider taking out a stakeholder pension for yourself or contribute to a stakeholder for a member of your family:

- **Tax benefits**
  For every £78 you put into your pension savings, the government puts in another £22 for basic rate tax payers. If you are a higher rate tax payer you will receive further tax relief through your tax code.
- **Non tax payer**
  Even if you are not in employment you can contribute to a stakeholder pension AND the government will top up any money that's put in, in the form of tax relief, and will currently let you have a tax-free lump sum when you draw the benefits from it.

This makes stakeholder a particularly attractive and tax efficient means of saving, for example, for a child, a homemaker with no income, or even a pensioner – and someone else can make contributions for you.

Am I eligible?
You are normally eligible for a stakeholder pension if you are a UK resident, under age 75 and you are:

- Self employed
- Employed – provided you are not in an occupational pension scheme where you earn more than £30,000 p.a. or where you are a controlling director
- Not working – e.g. homemaker or retired
- A child

There is also a maximum amount you can invest each year. Up to £3,600 can be paid to a plan annually, more may be allowable but further requirements have to be met.

Why buy online?
The main reason is simplicity:

- You don't need to send in any documents
- You don't need to sign any papers
- The form can be completed in as little as 5 minutes
- You just need your National Insurance and bank details to hand
- Price – by applying online you can usually benefit from lower charged products. For example, we only charge 0.8% for our stakeholder product – regardless of the size of your contribution.
- Managing your stakeholder – by applying online you will also be able to view and service your stakeholder online in many cases. For example, with our online stakeholder you will very shortly be able to view the current value, check your payment history, switch investment funds, update your name or address and change your bank details.

Who should I buy from?
Several companies offer stakeholder pensions but we believe that Friends Provident offers you the right solution for a number of reasons:

1) Award winning products

Friends Provident has won numerous awards over the years for our products. In particular we were the winner of the "Planned Savings Product and Service Excellence Award 2000" for Stakeholder Pensions.

Award winning products, backed up by an expert investment management team, has helped make Friends Provident one of today's leading financial providers.

2) Investment Expertise

The Friends Provident Group manages funds totalling around £37 billion world-wide. Our highly skilled fund managers will be working on your behalf aiming to provide you with above average investment returns

3) Technology

A few years ago we developed the highly automated systems that enabled us to become the first provider in the UK to meet stakeholder criteria. We have continued developing our technology so that our customers can get great service. For example, as an internet user, you will soon be able to call up a screen on your computer which gives an up to date overview of your finances, including the value of your stakeholder pension and the funds it is invested in. You will also be able to make changes to your pension while you are online.

To summarise, stakeholder pensions are simple, cheap and flexible pension plans offering significant tax benefits to everyone, working or not, aged from zero to 75 years old.

Friends Provident is a respected, long established financial services provider with bang up to date technology enabling you to start and manage your stakeholder pension online 24/7 – quickly, easily and cheaply.

FRIENDS tell it like it is

Visit Friends Provident Marketing Group at:

www.friendsprovident.com

Or phone us on 0870 607 1352

The value of a plan is not guaranteed and can go up and down depending on investment performance. Tax legislation may change. The value of any tax relief depends on your circumstances. Rates based on 2001/02 tax year.

Quoted source for the date:
Note 1: Office for National Statistics (www.statistics.gov.uk)

Certainly the best advice with pensions is to find out what you might end up with as far in advance as possible, and to review the situation regularly. All too often individuals leave checking up on pension entitlements or any planning to the years just before retirement – when it is generally too late to really change what you will get.

The other key tip is to start saving as much as possible as soon as possible – but that's a wider issue and not something specific to the internet.

The internet does already have useful educational material on pensions; over time as well the hope is that all parts of the pensions industry will improve their interactivity.

Information and education

State pensions

For state pensions, the government has set up the new Pensions Service, which in turn is part of the new Department of Work and Pensions. If you search for the old DSS, you will end up at the DWP (www.dwp.gov.uk). Both this and the related www.pensionguide.gov.uk ('the government's impartial pensions information site') have useful guides and information on all types of pensions. You can also fill out a claim form to get a forecast of your state pension.

Employer-based pensions

The internet capabilities of past or present employers will vary.

The Occupational Pensions Regulatory Authority (www.opra.gov.uk) (01273 627 600)
This is the watchdog for employer-based pensions. Opra also runs the Pension Schemes Registry, which helps trace old employer-based pension

entitlements (eg where a previous employer has been taken over by another company). You can fill out a tracing form online.

The Pensions Advisory Service (www.opas.org.uk) (0845 601 2923) OPAS is a non-profit organisation that gives free help and advice to people who have problems with their employer or personal pensions. Its website has a range of useful information.

The Financial Services Authority (www.fsa.gov.uk) has excellent information on pensions, including interactive 'decision tree' flowcharts.

Pension companies and brokers

Prudential (www.pru.co.uk)
Probably still Britain's biggest personal pensions company, the Pru allows stakeholder pension customers online access to their accounts. Also has annuity and retirement budgeting calculators.

Standard Life (www.standardlife.co.uk)
Britain's biggest mutual allows policyholders to get online pension fund values, make changes to and get other information on their pension plans.

Legal & General (www.landg.co.uk)
Allows online applications and plan management.

Virgin Money (www.virginmoney.com)
A very user-friendly website. You can apply for and invest in a stakeholder pension online; it also has calculators and other information.

Discount brokers for stakeholder pensions include:
www.discountpensions.co.uk
www.hargreaveslandsown.co.uk
www.bestinvest.co.uk

POINTON YORK
SIPP solutions
– self invested personal pension
the future in pension provision

SIPP's ought to be on the minds of all professionals from independent financial advisors, employee benefit consultants and employers, to individuals who want to have security, simplicity, flexibility, control and independence when planning for their retirement, using pensions.

Security – Within a SIPP the assets are held individually in the name of a trustee company. This segregation unlike an insured personal pension provides greater comfort should anything untoward happen to that Insurance Company.

Simplicity – The Self-Invested Personal Pension is simply a special variety of personal pensions, which can be used by both self employed and employed individuals (provided they are not earning pension benefits as members of an occupational scheme). It is a framework in which a wide range of investments options can be held; the individual is in control of those investments and may take advice from an advisor about the structure of those investments.

Flexibility – The benefits of a Self-Invested Personal Pension include flexibility of retirement benefits, and maximum control over the investments. The range of investments encompass Stocks and Shares traded on any recognised stock exchange (including the Alternative Investment Market, AIM), futures and Options, Unit Trusts and Investment Trusts, Open Ended Investment Companies, Insurance company managed funds, Endowment policies and deposit accounts, through to commercial property (including land whether development land, farmland or forestry) in or outside the UK.

Independence – The ability to keep the provider, the investment managers and the advisors separate gives the member greater independence and control and makes it easier to remove one element if it is not working out.

With a Pointon York SIPP you can:

- Take full control of your pension investments
- Use your full allocation of tax relief
- Invest in a wide range of vehicles
- Buy commercial property
- Begin to withdraw pension income and cash from the age of 50
- Transfer in your existing pension arrangements (we strongly recommend that you take professional advice on this)
- Benefit from:
  - Experienced staff who provide personal service
  - Transparent fees
  - Reduced fees for simultaneous application
  - Group SIPP, a scheme for the employees of an organisation
  - Total Pension Plan, a scheme which includes facilities to deal with earnings in excess of the cap
  - State of the art technology, which provides timely and meaningful information when required.

Pointon York Limited was established in 1971 by its current Chief Executive Geoffrey Pointon and has since then led the way in self-administered schemes.

Pointon York was one of the first to become a SIPP provider in 1990. It is regulated by the FSA and is an authorised institution under the Banking Act 1987.

Pointon York is based in Leicester and the City of London and is focussed on providing fee-based administration, trustee and technical support services. It is today the only independent UK SIPP provider who deals ONLY with SIPP's.

Contacts are:

Christine Hallett, *Managing Director*
0207 283 6240

Brian Donald, *Head of Business Development*
0207 283 6240

Mike Wilson, *Technical and Operations Director*
0116 255 1234

Charcolonline (www.charcolonline.co.uk) has an online stakeholder pension advice service and also allows online applications.

Sippdeal (www.sippdeal.co.uk) allows you to manage your Sipp (Self Invested Personal Pension) online.

Annuities

The Annuity Bureau (www.annuity-bureau.co.uk)
This contains excellent information explaining both pension and annuity types and has tables of best-buy annuities.

Annuity Direct (www.annuitydirect.co.uk)
This also has annuity guides and tables.

Moneyfacts (www.moneyfacts.co.uk)
This has annuity tables and other pension information.

Other

Help the Aged (www.helptheaged.org.uk)
Age Concern (www.ageconcern.org.uk)
Both campaign on behalf of pensioners (in the case of Age Concern, including a Your Rights week). Their websites also contain information on claiming benefits.

Saga (www.saga.co.uk)
Of older people's holiday fame, Saga also specialises in financial services for the over-50s, in particular insurance. This does not necessarily make it cheap, but its website does offer a range of advice, information and services for older people.

Traded endowment policies

In recent years there has been much criticism of endowment policies – once the most popular way of paying off a mortgage. Fears that many will not meet their home loan targets and claims that they are just plain poor value have encouraged more people – often foolishly – to cash them in before maturity.

Life insurers rarely give best value on policies 'surrendered' in this way. If you do want to cash in a policy, then it is worth investigating the market in 'secondhand' endowments. Policies can often be sold for more than the cash-in value offered by an insurer. The policies are bought up by others as lower risk investments.

The Association of Policy Market Makers (www.apmm.org)
The APMM promotes the secondhand policy market on behalf of its specialist member firms. Its website has explanations of what is involved and of much of the jargon-filled terminology of endowments. APMM member firms can be contacted directly, as follows:

Policy Plus	www.policyplus.com
Beale Dobie	www.bealedobie.co.uk/
1st Policy Company	www.1stpolicy.co.uk
Neville James	www.neville-james.co.uk
Policy Portfolio	www.policy.portfolio.co.uk
Foster & Cranfield Auctioneers	www.foster-and-cranfield.co.uk
Surrenda-Link	www.surrendalink.co.uk
Absolute Assigned Policies	www.aap.co.uk

11

Tax and Benefits

Tax

The government has said it wants to allow access to and deliver more services over the internet, and this includes filing tax returns. At the moment around 9 million people have to fill in a tax return each year – a chore that could do with any possible simplification.

The key advantage of completing your tax return online is that the software should do the calculation for you and automatically spot errors and discrepanciess, which you can then correct straight away.

In most cases it is already possible to complete and file returns via the Inland Revenue's own website (an important exception at the time of writing is people who have income from renting out property). However, so far only a small minority of people do so. Similarly, take-up of commercial software services has been low.

The government has not exactly gone out of its way to encourage taxpayers to go online by initially offering just a £10 discount for filing via the internet, and then taking even that discount away. Even so, the websites of the Revenue and other government departments do have excellent reference information on tax and benefits.

Inland Revenue (www.inlandrevenue.gov.uk)
The website for information about income and other taxes. Includes tax rates and thresholds, frequently asked questions (FAQs) and download-

able versions of the specialist tax leaflets normally available from Revenue offices. Also has contact details of local tax offices and a listing of helplines for particular tax areas. This website is also the starting point if you want to file your tax return online.

The Treasury (www.hm-treasury.gov.uk) also has more Budget documents.

Customs & Excise (www.hmce.gov.uk)
The Government department responsible for collecting VAT, the website has details on customs' allowances, duty on goods bought from foreign websites and VAT refunds for visitors to the UK.

TaxAid (www.taxaid.org.uk)
A tax charity that offers free help to people with tax questions or problems who can't afford an accountant. TaxAid will take questions by e-mail and its website also has plenty of useful guidance, including your rights as a taxpayer, what to do if you can't pay, and how to challenge a tax demand.

Digita (www.digita.com/taxcentral)
A leading tax software company, Digita's website has tax information, sample letters to download to better manage your tax affairs and many useful online calculators. These calculators include:

- Payslip Checker – check you are paying the correct amount of tax and National Insurance;
- Tax Code Checker – have you been assigned the correct Inland Revenue tax code?
- Student Loan Calculator – work out your repayments;
- Working Families Tax Credit Calculator – work out if you are entitled;
- Disabled Person's Tax Credit Calculator – find out if you or your partner are entitled;

When was the last time a website saved you thousands of pounds? **Taxsolve**, our **on-line tax advice** service offers an...

Grant Thornton 🍰

...accessible, user friendly, quick and easy way to receive high quality tax advice at the click of a button.

With representation in over 100 countries, you can rely on us to have the answer you need, however simple or complicated it is.

- free non obligation quote
- including international, personal and corporate tax advice
- value for money advice
- post your tax query any time day or night.

www.taxsolve.co.uk

- Children's Tax Credit Calculator – work out the amount of children's tax credit you are entitled to;
- Inheritance Tax Calculator – will your estate be liable for inheritance tax on your death?
- Bank Interest Calculator – calculate the net interest and related tax deduction on your bank accounts;
- Dividend Calculator – calculate the gross dividend received from shareholdings;
- Stamp Duty Calculator – calculate the amount of stamp duty charged when you buy property or shares;
- VAT Calculator – calculate the amount of VAT charged on goods or services.

Digita's website also has a free Online Tax Return service; it can also help you find a local tax adviser and sells software for people with more complicated tax affairs who need to fill in additional tax return forms.

Other online tax advice/tax filing services include:

E-Taxchecker	www.e-taxchecker.co.uk
Ascot Drummond (for small businesses)	www.ascotdrummond.co.uk
Tax Cafe	www.taxcafe.co.uk

Many of the big accountancy firms also have useful tax information on their websites, particularly at Budget time:

Arthur Andersen	www.arthurandersen.com
BDO Stoy Hayward	www.bdo.co.uk
Ernst & Young	www.ey.com
Grant Thornton	www.grant-thornton.co.uk
KPMG	www.kpmg.co.uk

Benefits

UK Online (www.ukonline.gov.uk)
The government's portal for all online services.

What used to be called the DSS at www.dss.gov.uk will take you through to the **Department for Work and Pensions** (www.dwp.gov.uk) which has full details of state benefits and how to claim.

Non-governmental organisations that will give information and/or advice on benefits include:

Child Poverty Action Group	www.cpag.org.uk
Citizens Advice Bureaux	www.nacab.org.uk
Local Law Centres	www.lawcentres.org.uk
(for free legal advice)	
National Council for One	www.oneparentfamilies.org.uk
Parent Families	
Shelter	www.shelter.org.uk

12

Utility Bills

With consumers' ability to choose their supplier of gas, electricity and phone – as well as internet ISP and mobile phone – utility bills are a whole lot more complicated nowadays. Rather than simply looking to keep consumption and therefore costs down, it is now possible to shop around for packages aimed at your own usage pattern. However competition has also led to massive 'confusion marketing' of these services, with different companies pricing in different ways, so making comparisons difficult.

The internet can help, not only in the basic research of tariffs from different companies but by actually working out the best deal for your usage. A range of broker-style services will calculate potential savings and identify better value suppliers based on you inputting your current bill details.

More utilities are also allowing account servicing over the internet – and in some cases offering discounts for customers prepared to deal this way. There appears no obvious reason why the internet shouldn't continue to grow in importance for the servicing and switching of basic utility bills and accounts.

Ofgem (Office of the Gas and Electricity Markets) (www.ofgem.gov.uk) The watchdog that regulates and promotes competition in the power industries. Ofgem's website has advice on switching suppliers and links to companies providing price comparison services.

Energywatch (www.energywatch.org.uk)
The gas and electricity consumer watchdog. Its information is even more focused at the individual, covering switching, price comparisons and complaints.

Oftel (Office of Telecommunications) (www.oftel.gov.uk)
Oftel is the regulator for phone, fax and internet industries. Website content includes information on the cost of calls on the internet, how to deal with junk faxes and telephone code changes.

Ofwat (Office of Water Services) (www.ofwat.gov.uk)
This is the equivalent body for the water industry.

Commercial price comparison services include:

www.uswitch.com
www.unravelit.com
www.buy.co.uk
www.saveonyourbills.co.uk
www.ukpower.co.uk

There is also useful advice on dealing with doorstep sellers – whether of energy or other services – on the website of Wigan Council's Trading Standards department at http://formby.wiganmbc.gov.uk/pub/ehcp/TS/consumer/doorstep.htm.

13

Watchdogs, Regulators and Trade Associations

It may educate, inform and even 'empower' consumers, but the internet will not stop scandals in the financial services industry. Indeed, it is more than likely it will breed new 'rip-offs'.

However, the web does give consumers easier access to the rules and regulations that are meant to govern the financial marketplace. A whole array of watchdogs, regulators and trade associations are on the internet. Many of their websites have useful generic information and guidance that should help protect consumers; others have search services – which purport to steer you in the direction of financial professionals rather than cowboys. At best these websites will be a resource for checking the claims of financial salespeople; equally consumers should be better able to resolve problems and complaints.

The Financial Services Authority (FSA) (www.fsa.gov.uk)
This is Britain's chief financial regulator, with a remit to educate consumers as well as police the financial services industry. Given most people's woefully low levels of financial understanding and the limited educational help given by regulators and industry in the past, the FSA's website is to be applauded. It has a whole range of useful tips, advice and guides, from how to choose an Isa to what to do if you are worried about your endowment.

You can also check online whether a financial firm is authorised to actually transact business. If a firm is not authorised you will not have recourse to the safety nets of the Financial Services Compensation Scheme (FSCS) and ombudsman (see below) should something go wrong.

The website also has comparative tables of financial products, which may help in shopping around.

The Financial Ombudsman Service (FOS) (www.financial-ombuds-man.org.uk)
The FOS arbitrates on problems with financial firms. It can award compensation, including in some cases for your time and trouble. The FOS is a free service for consumers and even if a ruling does not go in your favour, you can still take legal action. But rulings are binding on firms. It now incorporates most of the old financial omdudsmen schemes, including banking, insurance and investment.

The problems the FOS can normally help with are those relating to:

- banking services;
- credit cards issued by banks and building societies;
- endowment policies;
- financial and investment advice;
- health and loan protection insurance;
- household and buildings insurance;
- investment portfolio management;
- life assurance;
- mortgages;
- motor insurance;
- personal pension plans;
- private medical insurance;
- savings plans and accounts;
- stocks and shares;
- travel insurance;
- unit trusts and income bonds.

There is also a separate Pensions Ombudsman (www.pensions-ombuds-man.org.uk) who handles complaints about the way pension schemes are run (as opposed to the way pensions are sold or marketed, which falls under the FOS' remit).

Consumers can fill in an FOS complaint form online but for the ombudsman to look at a complaint you must first have reached deadlock with the firm you have a problem with.

The ombudsman's tips for complaining (taken from the FOS website) are:

1. It's usually best to complain to the firm in writing. If you phone, ask for the name of the person you speak to. Keep a note of this information, with the date and time of your call – and what was said. You may need to refer to this later.

2. Try to stay calm and polite, however angry or upset you are. You're more likely to explain your complaint clearly and effectively if you can stay calm.

3. If possible, start by contacting the person you originally dealt with. If they can't help, say you want to take matters further. Ask for details of the name or job title of the person who will be handling your complaint and for details of the firm's complaints procedure.

4. When you write a letter of complaint, write 'complaint' at the top. Set out the facts as clearly as possible. This will make it easier for the firm to start putting things right.

5. Write down the facts in a logical order and stick to what is relevant. Remember to include important details like your customer number or your policy or account number. Put these details at the top of your letter.

6. Keep a copy of any letters between you and the firm. You may need to refer to them later.

The Financial Services Compensation Scheme (www.fscs.org.uk)

This is a financial safety net for consumers. It compensates customers if a financial firm cannot pay claims against it, usually because it has gone out of business. The scheme, which is funded by the industry, covers investments, deposits and insurance. The website explains how to make a claim.

The Office of Fair Trading (OFT) (www.oft.gov.uk)

The OFT has been criticised for being ineffectual as a regulator, but its website does have useful information on consumer rights, including buying and selling property and taking out credit. There is also a section on online shopping rights and a 'Where to go for help' covering organisations to contact regarding specific consumer rights.

Consumers Association (www.which.net)

Unfortunately Which? magazine, the CA's well-known publication is only available for free over the internet on a trial basis – thereafter by subscription. Even so, the high quality of its consumer information makes it worthy of note.

The Consumer Gateway (www.dti.gov.uk/consumer_web)

This is run by the government's DTI and provides links to websites offering advice and information.

The British Bankers Association (BBA) (www.bba.org.uk)

Includes information on, for example, the cheque clearing process and checking charges.

The Banking Standards Board (www.bcsb.co.uk)

This is a key watchdog for the banking and savings industry. It is responsible for monitoring compliance with the Banking Code, which is aimed at ensuring customers get a fair deal.

The Council of Mortgage Lenders (CML) (www.cml.org.uk)

The CML has information on the mortgage market, buy-to-let, mortgage insurance, arrears and repossession.

The Association of British Insurers (ABI) (www.abi.org.uk)

This has some excellent practical information sheets on insurance issues.

WHO NEEDS ADVICE ?

If you know that you should use an Independent Financial Adviser (IFA), which type should it be? One that can offer you advice and find the right solutions, or one that can merely carry out your instructions and save you money by rebating most of their commissions?

If it's advice that you require, a good place to start is at www.Lewkay-Financial-Services.co.uk where you can get in touch with advisers that can offer bespoke advice and recommend solutions tailored to your requirements. Many years of experience are utilised to provide a first-class service to both private individuals and small to medium companies alike.

If you require a broker only to carry out your instructions and want to be rewarded for making your own decisions you need a good "discount broker" website where investments and protection plans can be discounted from any company offering it's products with commission to IFAs.

Discount Brokers have emerged from an era where investors have become more aware of the information available to them. The removal of the advice process by the broker has meant that the savings in time spent with a client can be passed-on in the form of big commission rebates - up to 90% of the initial commission at www.MaxValue.co.uk. See for yourself the savings that can be made. The best part is that there is no obligation, no pressure and nobody will contact you if you don't want them to.

INDEPENDENT FINANCIAL ADVICE

Do you have an endowment policy that you are thinking of surrendering or selling?

We are major brokers in the sale of unwanted endowment policies and can achieve big improvements over surrender values. All policies are put out to all of the UK's market makers in "second-hand" endowment policies. This makes us a one-stop-shop for anyone wishing to realise the capital in their policy. We do not buy the policies ourselves, but have access to all of the market makers that do. Why not try our secure online application service - it's free and you're under no obligation.

We also offer an "internet-only" financial services option to our clients, which enables us to rebate, on average, 80% of our initial commission. For example, a £25,000 Investment Bond would normally benefit from a further £1,040 of commission into the value of the plan.

If you are looking for any of the following, check out the discounts available

Investment Bonds	Life Assurance	Critical illness cover	ISAs
Pensions (Stakeholder, Personal, or company)		Ethical investments	
Ethical investments	Income Protection	PEP transfers	

The General Insurance Standards Council (www.gisc.co.uk)
The watchdog for the insurance industry.

Independent Financial Advisers (IFAs)

Online financial advice itself is largely a misnomer. Many financial websites offer information or guidance, but independent financial advisers (IFAs) would argue that, in most cases, this amounts to a lot less than the personalised advice you get from an IFA. Broadband internet may lead to IFAs offering advice delivered by videoconference, but for now Charcol www.charcolonline.co.uk is about the only online advice service. However you can find a local IFA via a number of websites:

IFA Promotion (www.unbiased.co.uk)
An organisation which promotes independent financial advice and advisers. As well as a free online search facility to find a local IFA, it produces some useful consumer factsheets and guides.

Institute of Financial Planning (www.financialplanning.org.uk)
The website of a group of financial advisers who call themselves 'planners'.

Society of Financial Advisers (www.sofa.org)
Sofa sets itself up as comprising 'top-end' financial advisers.

NB Some watchdogs and regulators are listed in other chapters as appropriate.

14

Internet and Finance Jargonbuster

The worlds of technology and finance both use more than their fair share of jargon. Sometimes this is a helpful shorthand, but jargon can also exclude and discourage consumers. In terms of technology, that means you may not get the most out of the brave new world of the internet – in terms of finance, it may cost you money. Here then is a combined jargonbuster of both internet and money terms to help your understanding of both.

Account – savings accounts need no explanation, but in the internet world an account also relates to a user's internet connection, such as AOL or Freeserve.

Account Aggregation Service – an internet service that enables (financial) accounts from different banks and companies to be shown on a single screen and accessed with just one set of security codes.

Additional Voluntary Contributions (AVCs) – a way of boosting a company pension. Like other pension plans you get tax relief. Free-standing AVCs are similar but sold by pension companies.

Address – electronic equivalent of a postal address; a string of words separated by dots, colons, slashes and other punctuation (but not spaces). Addresses are used to send or find information.

AER (annual equivalent rate) – standardised interest rate calculation that takes into account when interest is paid as well as the amount. Used with savings and current accounts in the same way that APR has been used for loans and credit cards.

All-risks – normally used in the context of an addition to a standard home insurance policy, giving cover for items while away from your property, for example a bicycle.

Alternative Investment Market (AIM) – a high risk stockmarket for small, growing companies.

Annual Percentage Rate (APR) – the interest rate on loans including all charges.

Annual Report – a yearly statement of a company's business and financial performance.

Annuity – an income that you get in exchange for a lump sum. With pension plans the annuity – the pension – pays out for the rest of your life.

Anti-Virus Software – special computer programs designed to intercept viruses (destructive programs) on your PC and stop them causing damage or to fix damage caused.

ASU Insurance – standing for Accident, Sickness and Unemployment, also called Payment Protection Insurance or Mortgage Payment Protection Insurance (MPPI). Covers loan repayments in the event of sickness or unemployment.

Bacs (Banks Automated Clearing System) – the main system for bank transfers, electronic credits and direct debits. Basically, it takes three working days – even over the internet! Banks continue to charge for same-day Chaps transfers.

Balance Sheet – a snapshot of a company's assets, debts and shareholder equity.

Bank of England – no you can't open an account! Sets interest rates on behalf of government.

Base Rate – the core level of interest rates; set by the Bank of England.

Basic State Pension – the main government-provided retirement benefit.

Bear – as opposed to bull. Investors who think prices are going to fall are bears, and if share prices are depressed it is said to be a bear market. Investors who think prices are on the up are bulls.

Blue Chip – shares of the biggest companies, named after the highest value gambling chip. Also a way of describing the big household name companies themselves.

Bonds – an over-used savings term but normally suggesting something lower risk. Strictly, bonds are debts of companies (corporate bonds) and governments (British government bonds are called Gilts) that can be bought and sold like shares. They normally pay a fixed rate of interest – hence they are also called fixed-interest securities – and mature at a fixed price. These bonds differ to those sold by building societies and insurers, which may give a return based on the performance of the stockmarket or pay interest rising in fixed steps.

Bricks and Clicks – describes a service available from both branch and over the internet. A traditional high street current account that also offers web access would be an example.

Broadband – high speed internet that will allow you to use the phone at the same time as being on the internet. Available now, broadband is the next big step in the development of internet usage. In finance, broadband could herald one-to-one videoconferencing with financial advisers for big, complicated or individualised transactions which to date have remained offline.

Broker – someone who sells financial products: a stockbroker sells shares, an insurance broker, insurance.

Browser – the computer program used for navigating or 'surfing' the web. Microsoft Internet Explorer and Netscape Navigator are the most widely used.

Building Society – like a bank but owned by its savers and borrowers. Some insurers are also 'mutuals'. In recent years a range of mutuals have paid windfalls as they have shed their mutual ownership structure.

Bulletin Board – also called a message board. Part of a website where users can leave messages that can be read by others.

Buy-to-let – a relatively new type of property investment where the investor plays landlord. The idea is the rent from tenants covers the mortgage, while the landlord also picks up any growth in the value of the property.

Capital Gains Tax (CGT) – a tax on investment profits such as a rise in the value of shares. But an investor's first £7,700 of capital gains each year is tax-free.

Capped Rate – a combination of a fixed and variable rate mortgage. Rates will never go above a certain level – the cap – and if rates fall, borrowers stand to benefit from a reduction in their home loan payments.

Carpetbagger – someone who opens an account or takes out a policy with a building society or mutual insurer primarily in the hope of a windfall.

Cashback Mortgage – a home loan that offers borrowers an upfront cash rebate for tying them in to a particular mortgage deal.

CAT Standard – a government benchmark for the Cost or Charges, Access and Terms of financial products. The idea was to provide reassurance to financial consumers that they were getting a fair deal, although CAT Standard products are often not the absolute best deal.

Chatroom – part of a website where users can send and receive messages instantly with others online at the same website.

Citizens Advice Bureaux – source of free help and advice on financial and other matters, including debt problems.

Completion Date – the day you get the keys and can move into your new home.

Content – an internet name for editorial news and features.

Conveyancing – the legal and administrative process in transferring the ownership of a property.

Credit Reference Agency – an organisation that lenders use to assess your creditworthiness. Keeps records of county court judgements (CCJs) for unpaid debts.

Critical Illness Insurance – a policy that pays out a lump sum if you suffer from, or are diagnosed with, one of a range of life-threatening conditions.

Cyberspace – the virtual space you're in when on the internet.

Daytrading – buying and selling shares in a very short timeframe (often a day or less, hence the name) with the aim of making a profit on very small price differences. Very high risk.

Death-in-service – life insurance provided as a benefit by an employer.

Defined Benefit Pension – a workplace-based scheme where your pension is based on years with an employer and salary at retirement or when you left; also called Final Salary.

Defined Contribution Pension – can be either a personal pension or a workplace scheme where the benefits depend on money put in and investment performance. Also called Money Purchase.

Demutualisation – when a mutual organisation, such as a building society, converts into a plc. Normally means windfalls for members. Conversion and demutualisation are often used interchangeably.

Digital Signature – a form of computer code that confirms your personal identity to others in electronic communications. Also called an electronic signature.

Discounted Variable Rate – a type of mortgage giving an initial discount against a lender's Standard Variable Rate (see below).

Dividends – the part of a company's profits distributed to shareholders, normally paid out half-yearly, also used to describe the income paid out by unit trusts.

Dot.com – a business that sells goods or services over the internet. Has turned into something of a term of abuse – as in 'dot.gone' or 'dot.con'.

E-commerce – buying and selling over the internet. Variations include e-banking and e-saving. E-cash is about internet payments.

E-mail – mail which is delivered electronically over the internet. Usually consists of text, but can contain illustrations, music and animations (normally as 'attachments'). Mail is sent to an e-mail address, which is the internet equivalent of a postal address.

Encryption – a process of scrambling information into an encoded form so that it can't be read while in transit on the internet. It can be read only by someone with the software to decode it.

Endowment – a combination of a life insurance and savings policy, usually sold with a mortgage. The endowment grows in value and, hopefully, pays off your home loan.

Equities – another name for shares. Like bonds, equities are issued by companies to raise money. Shareholders literally have equity in a company, and share in future risks and rewards.

Excess – the first part of a claim paid by a policyholder. If the amount of the loss is less than the excess, there is no point in claiming.

Exchange of Contracts – a legally binding agreement to buy and sell a property.

Final Salary Pension – another name for a Defined Benefit scheme.

Firewall – an internet security system that prevents access to certain web services (pornography, for example) from a particular PC.

Fixed Rate – as in a fixed rate bond or mortgage. The interest is known or guaranteed for a certain period, regardless of what happens to interest rates generally.

Flexible Mortgage – a home loan that, generally speaking, allows over- or underpayments of the normal monthly amount without penalty.

Freehold – absolute ownership of a property; as opposed to leasehold.

Freestanding AVC (FSAVC) – like an AVC, a way of boosting a company pension. FSAVC plans are sold by commercial pension companies. Most experts recommend Stakeholder Pensions as alternatives.

FTSE Indexes – for Financial Times Stock Exchange, such indexes are measures of the performance of stockmarkets and groups of shares and are benchmarks against which to measure the performance of your own investments. The FTSE 100 (or Footsie) measures the share price performance of the UK's 100 biggest companies. The FTSE All Share index also includes smaller companies.

Fully Comprehensive Cover – the top level of car insurance you can get, covering you for third party claims, fire and theft of your own vehicle, accidental damage etc.

Futures and Options – very high risk financial investments. Only for experts.

Gazumping – where a homebuyer's accepted offer for a property is pushed aside for a higher bid.

Gazundering – where a homebuyer reduces their agreed price at the last moment, knowing the seller is committed to moving.

Gearing – buy a flat for £100,000 with a deposit of £5,000 and the rest on a mortgage. A year later if the flat is worth £120,000 you've made 400 per cent on your original stake. That's gearing. But watch out: gearing can also work the other way, giving you disproportionate losses.

Gearing is also quite commonly used by investment trusts and is also built in to other high-risk investments.

Gilts – British government bonds.

Gross – an income payment that comes without tax deducted – as opposed to net.

HTML – the computer language used to create websites.

Income Multiple – the number of times of your annual salary a mortgage company will lend. Traditionally three times, but lenders are generally more flexible nowadays.

Income Protection Insurance – also called Permanent Health Insurance or PHI. Cover that replaces part of your income if you are unable to work because of illness or disability.

Index-Tracking – normally a unit trust, often in tax-free Isa form, which aims to match the performance of a particular stockmarket. Other, 'actively managed', funds set out to beat indexes (but many don't).

Individual Savings Account (Isa) – the government's tax-free investment plan which replaced Peps and Tessas. Currently, up to £7,000 can be invested in an Isa each year, of which a maximum £3,000 can be in cash savings. For most people the rest will be in unit or investment trusts.

Inflation – price increases, measured officially by the RPI or Retail Prices Index.

Interactive Television – a system that links your TV to the internet.

Interest-Only Mortgage – as opposed to Repayment. Can run stand-alone or with a separate repayment vehicle such as an endowment.

Internet – one or more computers connected to each other is, in effect, an internet (many offices have what they call an Intranet for internal use). The World Wide Web internet consists of a world-wide collection of interconnected computer networks.

Internet Café – also called cybercafes. These are public outlets where you can use internet-ready computers, usually for a fee based on the time you spend online.

Investment Trust – a type of investment fund in which you buy shares, as opposed to units in a unit trust. Investment trust shares can themselves exaggerate or dilute the performance of the fund's underlying investments.

ISP (Internet Service Provider) – service that connects you to the internet.

Leasehold – as opposed to freehold, in property: where ownership is only for a fixed number of years set by a lease.

Loan to Value (LTV) – used to compare mortgage and property value.

London Stock Exchange – the main UK stockmarket.

Mid-caps – not small companies but not FTSE 100 names either; the term is specifically used for the 250 next biggest companies after the FTSE 100 constituents.

Modem – a device that allows your computer to send (and receive) signals to and from a phone line and so connects you to the internet. Modems can be built into the computer or be external.

Money Purchase Pension – another name for a Defined Contribution pension.

Mutual – an organisation owned by its customers – called members – such as building societies and some insurers.

National Insurance – NI contributions are used in assessing entitlement to the basic state pension and Serps, as well as a number of other social security benefits.

Negative Equity – if your home is worth less than the amount of your outstanding mortgage then that difference is negative equity.

Non-Contributory Pension Scheme – where your employer alone pays in on your behalf; it costs you nothing.

Occupational Pensions – work-related; as opposed to state or personal pensions.

Open-Ended Investment Company (Oeic) – replacing unit trusts: a new type of investment fund.

Payment Protection Insurance – also called ASU insurance or Mortgage Payment Protection Insurance (MPPI). Covers monthly loan repayments if you are sick or lose your job.

Personal Pension Plan – a non-state, non-employer (normally), private pension. These have been criticised for high charges. New stakeholder pensions are aimed at reinstilling confidence in personal pension saving.

Portal – a website that is your first port of call when you go online. Often has news and information and contains a search engine.

Premium – the price you pay for insurance, or the amount you put in an insurance-linked investment.

Redemption Penalties – charges for paying off some or all of a mortgage or home loan, normally just during the first few years of a loan.

Remortgage – switching home loan deals without moving home.

Repayment Mortgage – where your monthly payment consists of both interest and a small part of the original debt. With this type of loan the original debt is gradually reducing all the time.

Repossession – until you pay off your mortgage, the lender has first claim on your home. Ultimately, if you stop paying the mortgage or get seriously behind on payments you face eviction by the lender. Once it has repossessed, the lender will resell the property to recover its money.

Search Engine – a program for finding websites using keywords.

Secure Connection – a way of sending encrypted information to (and from) a website. If you are using a secure connection, a symbol, usually a closed padlock, appears on your computer screen.

Serps (the State Earnings-Related Pension Scheme) – a 'second' state pension, with benefit levels more related to earnings than the basic state pension.

Shareholder – if you buy even one share in a company that makes you a shareholder. This entitles you to an invitation to the firm's annual general meeting (AGM) and to vote for directors and on other company matters.

Snail-mail – mail sent the old-fashioned way, with stamps. That said, many internet companies have not proved very efficient at responding to e-mails.

Stakeholder Pension – a low-cost pension plan brought in by the government, offered by both employers and pension companies.

Standard Variable Rate – a mortgage company's underlying home loan rate; the rate which home loan discounts are priced off.

Stock Exchange – another name for the stockmarket, where shares (also called stock) are bought and sold.

Stockbroker – someone who advises on shares, and buys and sells them for you.

Stockmarket – see Stock Exchange.

Sub-Prime – lending to people with a poor credit history.

Takeover – an offer to buy the shares of a company by another company. Normally good news for shareholders in the takeover target.

Term Assurance – life insurance which pays out if you die within a specified period (the 'term').

Third Party Insurance Cover – the basic, legally required car insurance. Covers you for damage to other people and their cars and property.

Unit Trust – a type of investment fund which, by putting money in a range of shares and bonds, reduces the risk from any one investment turning out bad. The most popular type of stockmarket Isa investment.

Valuation – of a property; a requirement of lenders to check whether property is adequate security for their loan.

Venture Capital – investment in a new or developing business that does not yet have shares tradeable on a stockmarket.

Virus – destructive computer program designed to infect and often damage other computer programs. Can alter and delete data and send data to other computers.

Wall Street – another name for the US stockmarket and part of New York's financial district. Actually not as impressive as London's Canary Wharf or other parts of the City of London.

Wap – Wireless Application Protocol, a much-talked about mobile phone technology for accessing the internet. Wap phone services have not been popular or successful.

Web page – document which forms part of a website.

Website – a collection of related web pages that typically belong to an organisation and are about the same subject.

With-profits – a form of indirect stockmarket investment where returns are in the form of bonuses awarded by the insurance company managing the investment.

Windfall – most commonly used term to describe payouts from demutualising building societies and insurers.

World Wide Web – another name for the internet.

Yield – the annual dividend or income expressed as a percentage of the value of an investment.

Index of Advertisers